Beliefs
Important to
Baptists

STUDY GUIDE

BAPTISTWAY®

Dallas, Texas

BAPTISTWAY PRESS® Management Team
Executive Director, Baptist General Convention of Texas: Charles Wade
Coordinator, Church Health and Growth Section: H. Lynn Eckeberger
Director, Bible Study/Discipleship Center: Dennis Parrott
Administrator, Curriculum Development Office: Bernard M. Spooner

Publishing consultant: Ross West, Positive Difference Communications
Cover and Interior Design and Production: Desktop Miracles, Inc.

ISBN: 1–931060–18–5

Beliefs Important to Baptists

Beliefs Important to Baptists

This *Study Guide* is intended to provide guidance and content as you study the biblical bases of some beliefs that are important to Baptists. The twelve beliefs to be studied are listed alphabetically on the preceding page after an introductory lesson, "Who in the World Are Baptists, Anyway?" The lessons provide studies of twelve beliefs important to Baptists. This list of basic Baptist beliefs is not an "official" list, but the beliefs listed are representative of what many Baptists believe.

The twelve Baptist beliefs to be studied are listed and published in alphabetical order so as not to suggest an "official" listing of beliefs from more important to less important. In studying these Baptist beliefs, you are encouraged to study first, "Who in the World Are Baptists, Anyway?" After that, the twelve beliefs important to Baptists can be studied in any order.

You will note that this study is a Bible study. The intention of these study materials is that you study the Bible carefully with the aid of these comments as you seek to understand these beliefs important to Baptists.

Who in the World Are Baptists, Anyway?

BACKGROUND SCRIPTURES

Genesis 1:26–27; Matthew 16:13–17;
John 3:1–16; Ephesians 2:1–19

FOCAL TEXT

Ephesians 2:1–19

MAIN IDEA

"The doctrine of the soul's competency in religion under God is the historical significance of the Baptists"[1] and means that God provides each person with the ability and freedom to make decisions in matters relating to God.

STUDY AIM

To summarize some basic biblical understandings that are the source of who Baptists are, what they believe, and how they live

QUICK READ

This lesson provides an introduction to the biblical basis for principles that describe what it means to be a Baptist Christian with a primary emphasis on soul competency before God.

Baptists frequently make the headlines and the newscasts. Some of the stories are positive, such as those about Baptist relief efforts in the midst of disasters. Unfortunately, other stories paint Baptists as "feuding, fussing, and fighting" most of the time. People who are not Baptists wonder, "Who in the world are Baptists, anyway?" In fact, a number of Baptists seem to wonder the same thing!

To further complicate matters, people with very diverse beliefs and actions wear the name "Baptist." For example, Lester Maddox, the former segregationist governor of Georgia, and Martin Luther King, Jr., the leader of the civil rights movement, were both Baptists. Walter Rauschenbush, the theologian for the social gospel movement, and Billy Graham, the world's best-known evangelist, both are part of the Baptist family of Christians. Baptists can be found in various political parties in our nation. Baptists advocate a wide variety of views on social and moral issues. Baptists hold differing convictions about theology and interpretation of the Bible.

So what makes a Baptist a Baptist? And why are Baptists so diverse? Those are difficult questions without simple answers. In fact, no single doctrine or belief can describe what it means to be a Baptist. Much like a recipe, a combination of doctrines and beliefs actually go into describing a Baptist. And people hold different ideas about what should go into the Baptist mix. Yet most Baptists agree on the core ingredients. This lesson will explore the biblical foundation for a number of these basic Baptist beliefs, recognizing that such a brief space provides only for a limited discussion.

Soul Competency (Ephesians 2:1–7)

The Holy Spirit led Paul, the great missionary of the first century, to write to the Christians at Ephesus about their life in Christ. He emphasized that apart from Christ there is no salvation from sin and death. Paul also stressed that each person possesses the capacity to decide whether to

Ephesians 2:1–19 (NIV)

[1]As for you, you were dead in your transgressions and sins, [2]in which you used to live when you followed the ways of this world and of the ruler of the kingdom of the air, the spirit who is now at work in those who are disobedient. [3]All of us also lived among them at one time, gratifying the cravings of our sinful nature and following its desires and thoughts. Like the rest, we were by nature objects of wrath. [4]But because of his great love for us, God, who is rich in mercy, [5]made us alive with Christ even when we were dead in transgressions—it is by grace you have been saved. [6]And God raised us up with Christ and seated us with him in the heavenly realms in Christ Jesus, [7]in order that in the coming ages he might show the incomparable riches of his grace, expressed in his kindness to us in Christ Jesus. [8]For it is by grace you have been saved, through faith—and this not from yourselves, it is the gift of God—[9]not by works, so that no one can boast. [10]For we are God's workmanship, created in Christ Jesus to do good works, which God prepared in advance for us to do.

[11]Therefore, remember that formerly you who are Gentiles by birth and called "uncircumcised" by those who call themselves "the circumcision" (that done in the body by the hands of men)—[12]remember that at that time you were separate from Christ, excluded from citizenship in Israel and foreigners to the covenants of the promise, without hope and without God in the world. [13]But now in Christ Jesus you who once were far away have been brought near through the blood of Christ.

[14]For he himself is our peace, who has made the two one and has destroyed the barrier, the dividing wall of hostility, [15]by abolishing in his flesh the law with its commandments and regulations. His purpose was to create in himself one new man out of the two, thus making peace, [16]and in this one body to reconcile both of them to God through the cross, by which he put to death their hostility. [17]He came and preached peace to you who were far away and peace to those who were near. [18]For through him we both have access to the Father by one Spirit.

[19]Consequently, you are no longer foreigners and aliens, but fellow citizens with God's people and members of God's household . . . .

follow Jesus or not. He indicated that the Ephesian Christians through faith in Christ had determined to leave the ways of the world (2:2–3), to respond to God's love in Christ, and to live lives worthy of heaven (2:4–7). Throughout this letter Paul indicated that the Ephesians had choices to make, such as his appeal to "live a life worthy of the calling you have received" (4:1).

Paul based his assumption that the Ephesians possessed the ability to respond to his appeals solidly on the writings of the Old Testament and the teachings of the Lord Jesus Christ. Genesis reveals that God created human beings with the freedom of choice (Genesis 1:26–27). The Old Testament prophets called on the people of Israel to turn from their wicked ways to God's ways. Jesus' initial preaching urged people to repent. Moreover, Jesus asked Peter to make a personal decision regarding

George W. Truett and Religious Liberty

Many historians consider George W. Truett, pastor of the First Baptist Church in Dallas from 1898 to 1944, as one of the greatest, if not the greatest, pastor in Southern Baptist life. Never provincial in his outlook, he served as president of both the Southern Baptist Convention and of the Baptist World Alliance. He also gave strong support to the Baptist General Convention of Texas and to institutions related to the convention. When Truett died, the entire Dallas community expressed love and appreciation for him. City and county offices were closed in his honor, and a huge crowd attended his funeral.

In 1920 Truett delivered one of the most famous sermons in Baptist history from the east steps of the Capitol in Washington, D. C. His theme was religious liberty. In the sermon, he quoted Jesus' statement, "Render unto Caesar the things which are Caesar's, and unto God the things that are God's" (Matthew 22:21, KJV). He then declared: "That utterance, once and for all, marked the divorcement of church and state."[3]

who Jesus was (Matthew 16:13–17). These appeals for people to decide for God would be cruel farces if human beings did not have the capacity to choose to respond.

Therefore a basic Baptist belief is "the doctrine of the soul's competency in religion under God."[2] This belief is not an emphasis on human self-sufficiency. Rather, it stresses that the ability to decide—that is, the competency of the soul—is a gift from God. Thus we have freedom of choice because God has so gifted us. Furthermore, the choice cannot be delegated. Each person must decide for herself or himself to follow Jesus or not. No one can make that choice for another. Baptists declare that no one should try to coerce another in a decision for Christ. Neither church nor government, Baptists believe, has any right to attempt to force a religious decision on anyone. Certainly Baptists seek to persuade people to follow Christ, but they realize that such commitment is a voluntary individual decision.

Many Baptists believe that the doctrine of soul competency is basic to other Baptist beliefs. It relates to many other doctrines that Baptists cherish, in a sense tying them together.

Salvation by Grace Through Faith (Eph. 2:8–10)

The Bible teaches that salvation is in Christ by grace through faith alone. This certainly relates to soul competency. Paul stated to the Ephesians: "For it is by grace you have been saved, through faith—and this not from yourselves, it is the gift of God—not by works, so that no one can boast" (2:8–9). Baptists believe in the deity and lordship of Jesus Christ. Baptists insist that salvation from sin and death to forgiveness and life is only found in Jesus Christ, who declared, "I am the way and the truth and the life. No one comes to the Father except through me" (John 14:6).

God's grace—God's unmerited love for lost humanity—led God to send his Son to be our Savior. As Jesus told Nicodemus, the Jewish leader who came to him by night, "For God so loved the world that he gave his one and only Son, that whoever believes in him shall not perish but have eternal life" (John 3:16). Baptists believe that it is grace/faith plus nothing that results in salvation—not grace/faith plus good works, or church membership, or baptism, or sacrament, or anything else. People are free to believe or not to believe in Jesus as personal Lord and Savior. Those who believe in Jesus as Savior pass from death that is the result of sin to eternal and abundant life that is the result of faith in Christ. Baptists declare also that this salvation is secure for eternity in Christ.

Each believer is to express through believer's baptism, another major belief of Baptists, that he or she has been made "alive with Christ" (Eph. 2:5). Both words are important: *believer's* and *baptism*. Baptists declare that only those who have personally made a decision to believe in Christ should be baptized because only through belief do we pass from death to life as is symbolized in baptism. That is why Baptists reject infant baptism. The word *baptize* means to immerse. Therefore, Baptists immerse believers as a beautiful picture of their death to an old way of life and being "raised . . . up with Christ" (2:6). Baptism also enables the believer to identify with the death, burial, and resurrection of Jesus. Baptism is a symbol of what has taken place in the person through belief in Christ. Baptism does not save but is a picture of salvation. It is also a covenant with God and with fellow believers to live worthy of Christ. Similarly, Baptists believe that the Lord's Supper is not a sacrament or necessary for salvation but symbolizes the broken body and shed blood of Jesus for our salvation.

Baptism takes place within the community of believers, a church. Paul wrote to the Ephesians about people of diverse background, such as Jews and Gentiles, being brought together as one in Christ. Thus, a church is to be made up of people who have "been brought near through the blood of Christ" (2:13). As such, a church is a divine-human organization. It is divine in the sense that it is the "body of Christ" and only those who have been saved in Christ are to be members. It is human in that it is made up of people who are saved but who are still imperfect.

Another way to state this conviction is that Baptists hold to the concept of a "believers' church," a regenerate church membership. Only people who have been saved by grace through faith and who have testified to that experience are to be members of a church. This means that each member of the local body of baptized believers has come into the fellowship in the same way. There is equality in salvation and church membership.

This leads to the Baptist emphasis on *theo-democratic* church governance. Baptist churches have no hierarchy. No individual or group of people decides for the entire body of members what they are to believe and to do. Rather each member of the body shares in the decisions. Yet, ideally, the decisions are not to be what the people want, but what Christ, the head of the church, wants. Thus the use of the term *theo-* (the Greek word for God) *democracy* (the word for rule by the people). Through Bible study, prayer, discussion, and meditation the members are to seek the will of God as they participate in congregational church governance.

Furthermore, each church is autonomous—that is, independent. Baptist churches are not subject to rule or governance by any outside body in regard to faith and religious practice. No "denominational headquarters" or government agency dictates to a church what to believe or how to worship. How could it be otherwise? The Bible indicates that each believer is competent in religion under God. Therefore each church made up of Baptists is equal before God and has no authority over another.

However, a local body of baptized believers on its own cannot adequately carry out the Great Commission of the Lord Jesus Christ (Matthew 28:18–20). Therefore, Baptist churches cooperate with one another for the sake of missions, evangelism, Christian education, ministry, and other causes. This cooperation is purely voluntary, as it was in New Testament times among churches. Voluntary cooperation among Baptist churches began with associations of churches, expanded to state conventions, and finally to national conventions and bodies of Baptists.

Each church relates directly to any organization of Baptists beyond it, and that relationship is always voluntary. Baptist organizations beyond local congregations are also autonomous and relate voluntarily with one another. Through such voluntary cooperation, Baptists have been able to have an impact for good on millions of people throughout the world.

Priesthood of the Believers (Eph. 2:11–19)

Saved by grace through faith and competent in religion under God, each Baptist through Christ has "access to the Father by one Spirit" (2:18). Paul declared to the Ephesians that each believer in Christ has access to God in the same way. There is not one way for the Gentile and another for the Jew. In Christ such distinctions disappear, and every believer has equal access to God.

The New Testament reveals that in Christ we become "priests." Peter stated that those in Christ are a "holy priesthood" (1 Peter 2:5) and a "royal priesthood" (1 Peter 2:9). In the Old Testament the people had access to God through priests. In the New Testament every disciple of Jesus has access to God directly. Thus a major emphasis of Baptists is the "priesthood of believers."

Being a priest carries both opportunity and responsibility. The opportunity is to relate directly with God through prayer, worship, meditation, trust, and obedience. No special clerical class is needed to represent us to God or to serve as a mediator between God and ourselves. However, with this opportunity goes responsibility. We are to take the knowledge of God that is ours and share it with everyone in witness and ministry. That is, we are to be priests to others, loving and caring for them in Jesus' name. Therefore, Baptists take seriously their individual responsibility for evangelism, mission, and ministry to all people.

The doctrine of the priesthood of believers coupled with the doctrine of soul competency calls for religious freedom and the separation of

Beliefs Important to Baptists

The Baptist Distinctives Committee of the Baptist General Convention of Texas has developed a list of basic Baptist beliefs that are considered not "official" but representative of what many Baptists believe. In alphabetical order, not by priority, these are the beliefs:

Authority of the Bible
Autonomy of the local congregation of believers
Believer's baptism and church membership
Congregational church government
Deity and lordship of Jesus Christ
Evangelism and missions: the Great Commission
Religious freedom and separation of church and state
Salvation only by grace through faith
Security of the believer
Soul competency and the priesthood of the believer
Symbolic understanding of baptism and the Lord's Supper
Voluntary cooperation among churches

church and state. Under God, people ought to be free to exercise both their competency in matters of faith and religious practice as well as their opportunity and responsibility as believer priests. No ecclesiastical or governmental body ought to interfere with these practices or attempt to dictate to the followers of Christ what to believe or how to respond to what they perceive as the will of God.

When Baptists first proclaimed religious liberty, they met terrible resistance. Religious authorities viewed the concept as heretical. Governmental authorities viewed it as treasonous. They thought that allowing people religious freedom would weaken the power of the government and possibly cause people to demand political as well as religious freedom. Baptists were seen as a threat both to despotic monarchs and to dictatorial clergy. Therefore Baptists suffered persecution at the hands of both

church and state. Ridicule, abuse, imprisonment, torture, and death did
not silence the Baptists, however. They persisted in their struggle for religious freedom for all, not just for themselves.

Largely due to the efforts of Baptists and others of similar views, we
enjoy religious freedom in the United States. The Bill of Rights in the
Constitution of the United States guarantees that our nation will have no
established—that is, government-supported—religion. In many places in
the world, governments support a particular religion or Christian denomination in various ways, such as through taxation. Baptists insist that the
support of a church ought to be by the voluntary tithes and offerings of
the members, not by government-coerced taxation.

We can be grateful that church and state are separate in our nation,
with churches supported voluntarily by members and not through government coercion. People of all religious persuasions and those with none
are to be free from government interference in matters of faith. Soul competency and the priesthood of believers are best practiced when there is a
free church in a free state

So Who in the World Are Baptists, Anyway?

Basic to all of these beliefs is the Baptist insistence that the Bible is the
Word of God and our sole written authority for faith and practice. Baptists declare that we have no creed but the Bible. Baptists reject all creeds
as spurious efforts to capture the truth of the Holy Bible in a human document. Indeed, Baptists have developed confessions of faith, but these are
intended to serve only as broad guides to interpretation and never as an
authoritative or official expression of biblical truth. Such confessions are
merely that—confessions of what a particular group of Baptists believe.
They have no authority over any individual or church.

Thus we return to a core Baptist conviction: freedom of the soul before
God. This freedom includes freedom to interpret the Bible. With that

freedom goes responsibility, of course, such as the responsibility to seek the guidance of the Holy Spirit in interpreting Scripture and to use sound principles of biblical interpretation.

So who in the world are Baptists, anyway? Certainly we have much in common with all followers of Jesus Christ, such as a belief in God, the Bible, Jesus, and the importance of church. However, we differ on certain matters and emphasize particular doctrines. These differences and emphases taken as a whole set Baptists apart as distinctive. We believe these beliefs that define us are based on the Bible. We also believe that each person ought to be free to determine his or her own beliefs apart from coercion of church or state. Thus Baptists share enthusiastically our view of God, salvation, and other key doctrines while granting to others the freedom to share their views. In fact, Baptists have been willing to die for the freedom of all people to express through word and deed their religious convictions. That is a heritage worth preserving for the generations to follow.

QUESTIONS

1. Consider the list in the sidebar, "Beliefs Important to Baptists," set forth by the Baptist Distinctives Committee of the Baptist General Convention of Texas. Would you add any? Take away? (You may want to plan to continue your study of these beliefs through the three Bible study units in the series *Beliefs Important to Baptists*.)

2. Why is the concept of soul competency basic to many of the other Baptist doctrines?

3. Which of the Baptist beliefs and doctrines would you describe as the most basic and why?

4. Some people believe that the sovereignty of God rules out the freedom of choice in human beings. How do you respond to this?

5. What evidence, if any, do you see that some Baptist bodies today are endeavoring to dictate to other Baptist bodies what to believe? What basic Baptist beliefs would such practices violate?

6. How would you describe what it means to be a Baptist to someone who is not a Baptist?

NOTES

1. E. Y. Mullins, *Axioms of Religion,* Baptist Classics Series (Nashville: Broadman and Holman, Publishers, 1997), 66.
2. Mullins, 66.
3. The full text of George W. Truett's sermon, "Baptists and Religious Liberty," can be accessed on the internet at this address: http://www.bjcpa.org/pubs/fultruet.html

The Authority of the Bible

BACKGROUND SCRIPTURES

Psalm 19:7–10; 119:11, 97–112; Isaiah 40:8; Jeremiah 36; Matthew 5:17–18; Luke 21:33; 24:13–49; Acts 17:10–12; Romans 15:4; 2 Timothy 3:14–17; Hebrews 4:12–13; 2 Peter 1:19–21

FOCAL TEXTS

Psalm 119:97–112; Luke 24:13–45; Romans 15:4; 2 Timothy 3:14–17; 2 Peter 1:19–21

MAIN IDEA

" . . . The authority of the Bible is the authority of Christ. . . . Christ speaks to us through the Bible. Our ultimate authority in Christianity is the authority of Christ as the revelation of God."[1]

STUDY AIM

To describe how the Scriptures are authoritative for our lives

QUICK READ

Authority establishes truth and prescribes practice. Baptists accept the Bible as authority because it is God's revelation in Jesus Christ and can therefore guide in all Christian belief and behavior.

It was a Sunday evening church training period, and somehow I unex-
pectedly found myself as the youth teacher. Trying to be relevant, I asked
the group what they would like to talk about. One young woman declared
that she would like to talk about interracial marriage.

"Ok," I said, "What do you think about it?"

"Well," she answered, "we know it is wrong because the Bible says it is!"

"And where does the Bible say that?" I asked.

"I don't know," she rejoined, "but I know it does because I have always
been told it does."

We began to try to find what the Bible actually says about interracial
marriage. We looked at Deuteronomy 7:3–4; Ezra 9:1—10:44; and
Nehemiah 10:28–30. We found that in every case, the prohibition of
marriage with other peoples was based on religious factors, not racial.
"Do not intermarry with them . . . for they will turn your sons away from
following me to serve other gods" (Deut. 7:3–4).

What had been the problem? This fine young woman was allowing
what she had always been told to serve as the authority for what she
believed. Authority for believers rests in the Word of God, not in any
other source.

In a religious sense, authority is that which establishes belief and
guides conduct. Russell H. Dilday, Jr., defines authority as "*that right or
power to command action or compliance or to determine belief or custom in
matters of religion.*"[2] Some people and groups base their authority on inadequate sources such as tradition, the church, culture, worldview, reason,
creeds, prestigious people, or even personal experience. Christians consider Scripture, rather than such inadequate sources, to be their full
authority.

Baptists consider the Bible authoritative for all they believe and everything they should do. The Bible remains and will remain "the supreme
standard by which all human conduct, creeds, and religious opinions
should be tried."[3] Scripture constitutes the authority for Baptists because
it is God's revelation of his truth and his will.

Psalm 119:97–112 (NIV)

97 Oh, how I love your law!
 I meditate on it all day long.
98 Your commands make me wiser than my enemies,
 for they are ever with me.
99 I have more insight than all my teachers,
 for I meditate on your statutes.
100 I have more understanding than the elders,
 for I obey your precepts.
101 I have kept my feet from every evil path
 so that I might obey your word.
102 I have not departed from your laws,
 for you yourself have taught me.
103 How sweet are your words to my taste,
 sweeter than honey to my mouth!
104 I gain understanding from your precepts;
 therefore I hate every wrong path.
105 Your word is a lamp to my feet
 and a light for my path.
106 I have taken an oath and confirmed it,
 that I will follow your righteous laws.
107 I have suffered much;
 preserve my life, O LORD, according to your
 word.
108 Accept, O LORD, the willing praise of my mouth,
 and teach me your laws.
109 Though I constantly take my life in my hands,
 I will not forget your law.
110 The wicked have set a snare for me,
 but I have not strayed from your precepts.
111 Your statutes are my heritage forever;
 they are the joy of my heart.
112 My heart is set on keeping your decrees
 to the very end.

It is one thing for Christians as a whole or as a group (such as Baptists) to affirm the Bible as authoritative. It is another for you as an individual, however, to make the Bible God's ultimate authority for your belief and behavior. This lesson centers on the question, "How can the Bible become the central authority in your life?"

Luke 24:13–45

[13]Now that same day two of them were going to a village called Emmaus, about seven miles from Jerusalem. [14]They were talking with each other about everything that had happened. [15]As they talked and discussed these things with each other, Jesus himself came up and walked along with them; [16]but they were kept from recognizing him.

[17]He asked them, "What are you discussing together as you walk along?"

They stood still, their faces downcast. [18]One of them, named Cleopas, asked him, "Are you only a visitor to Jerusalem and do not know the things that have happened there in these days?"

[19]"What things?" he asked.

"About Jesus of Nazareth," they replied. "He was a prophet, powerful in word and deed before God and all the people. [20]The chief priests and our rulers handed him over to be sentenced to death, and they crucified him; [21]but we had hoped that he was the one who was going to redeem Israel. And what is more, it is the third day since all this took place. [22]In addition, some of our women amazed us. They went to the tomb early this morning [23]but didn't find his body. They came and told us that they had seen a vision of angels, who said he was alive. [24]Then some of our companions went to the tomb and found it just as the women had said, but him they did not see."

[25]He said to them, "How foolish you are, and how slow of heart to believe all that the prophets have spoken! [26]Did not the Christ have to suffer these things and then enter his glory?" [27]And beginning with Moses and all the Prophets, he explained to them what was said in all the Scriptures concerning himself.

[28]As they approached the village to which they were going, Jesus acted as if he were going farther. [29]But they urged him strongly, "Stay

with us, for it is nearly evening; the day is almost over." So he went in to stay with them.

[30]When he was at the table with them, he took bread, gave thanks, broke it and began to give it to them. [31]Then their eyes were opened and they recognized him, and he disappeared from their sight. [32]They asked each other, "Were not our hearts burning within us while he talked with us on the road and opened the Scriptures to us?"

[33]They got up and returned at once to Jerusalem. There they found the Eleven and those with them, assembled together [34]and saying, "It is true! The Lord has risen and has appeared to Simon." [35]Then the two told what had happened on the way, and how Jesus was recognized by them when he broke the bread.

[36]While they were still talking about this, Jesus himself stood among them and said to them, "Peace be with you."

[37]They were startled and frightened, thinking they saw a ghost. [38]He said to them, "Why are you troubled, and why do doubts rise in your minds? [39]Look at my hands and my feet. It is I myself! Touch me and see; a ghost does not have flesh and bones, as you see I have."

[40]When he had said this, he showed them his hands and feet. [41]And while they still did not believe it because of joy and amazement, he asked them, "Do you have anything here to eat?" [42]They gave him a piece of broiled fish, [43]and he took it and ate it in their presence.

[44]He said to them, "This is what I told you while I was still with you: Everything must be fulfilled that is written about me in the Law of Moses, the Prophets and the Psalms."

[45]Then he opened their minds so they could understand the Scriptures.

Romans 15:4

For everything that was written in the past was written to teach us, so that through endurance and the encouragement of the Scriptures we might have hope.

2 Timothy 3:14–17

[14]But as for you, continue in what you have learned and have become convinced of, because you know those from whom you learned it, [15]and how from infancy you have known the holy Scriptures, which are able to make you wise for salvation through faith in Christ Jesus. [16]All Scripture is God-breathed and is useful for teaching, rebuking, correcting and training in righteousness, [17]so that the man of God may be thoroughly equipped for every good work.

2 Peter 1:19–21

[19]And we have the word of the prophets made more certain, and you will do well to pay attention to it, as to a light shining in a dark place, until the day dawns and the morning star rises in your hearts. [20]Above all, you must understand that no prophecy of Scripture came about by the prophet's own interpretation. [21]For prophecy never had its origin in the will of man, but men spoke from God as they were carried along by the Holy Spirit.

Leading to Personal Faith in Christ (Luke 24:13–45)

Scripture will become the central authority in your life only as the Bible's message leads you to personal relationship with Jesus. God the Father remains the one supreme, eternal, and all-knowing Being and therefore the ultimate source of authority. He has, however, revealed himself, his nature and will, through his Spirit in the person of his Son Jesus Christ.[4] Russell Dilday summarizes these truths in these words: "Our authority then is the sovereign, triune God, revealed in Jesus Christ, communicated through his inspired Word, and confirmed by the Holy Spirit in Christian experience."[5]

The account of the disciples on the road to Emmaus (Luke 24:13–45) demonstrates how God's Word leads believers to personal relationship with Jesus and through that experience to apprehend and practice biblical truth. On the day of Jesus' resurrection, these disciples were traveling from Jerusalem to the village of Emmaus. They were discussing the events of Jesus' death. They spoke of reports of the missing body. Jesus joined the two, but God prevented them from recognizing him.

Jesus entered into their conversation. Cleopas revealed his and his friend's hesitation to affirm either belief or disbelief in Jesus' promise of resurrection. They reported that "some of our women" (24:22) said they did not find the body at the tomb but rather saw a vision of angels who said Jesus was alive. The two also reported that the apostles had found the grave empty. The Emmaus-bound disciples expressed their dimming hope that Jesus was Messiah (the redeemer of Israel). Three days had passed since the cross. They felt that if Jesus had been Messiah, it would have been confirmed by this time.

Saying they were "slow of heart" to believe the prophets' words (24:25), Jesus unfolded the biblical teachings. Beginning with "Moses and all the Prophets" (24:27), Jesus explained to them what the Scriptures taught about the Christ—that the death of Messiah was predicted as part of God's redemptive plan. The prophecies taught, said Jesus, that the Messiah (Christ), by divine necessity, had to suffer the agonies of betrayal, mockery, and death before entering his glory.

Jesus paused and ate with the struggling believers. As Jesus blessed the bread, their eyes were opened. They recognized the Master! Jesus then vanished from their sight. They exclaimed to each other, "'Were not our hearts burning within us while he talked with us on the road and opened the Scriptures to us?'" (24:32).

All doubt was erased after Jesus explained to them the message of the Scriptures. The disciples immediately returned to Jerusalem, unafraid of the danger of night travel. They proclaimed their experience to the apostles and other disciples who also were testifying that Jesus had indeed risen. Understanding the message of Scripture led these disciples to a new faith and relationship with Christ.

The Bible becomes authoritative for you today when you, too, allow Scripture to draw you to an experience with Jesus. For believers, Jesus

becomes more than a historical person, though he is certainly that. Jesus
becomes the living Lord who saves, directs, and guides. Jesus, whose will
is revealed in the Scriptures, constitutes authority. The Bible becomes
authoritative when the Holy Spirit through Scripture makes Christ
known in experience. Do you desire the Bible to guide and help you
more? The Bible will become more authoritative for you as you experience Christ through the Bible's message.

Understanding the Nature
of Scripture (2 Timothy 3:14–17)

Scripture will become the central authority for your life as you comprehend and accept the true nature of Scripture. The true nature of Scripture
includes Scripture's divine origin, its incredible unity, its miraculous
preservation, its incredible power, its continuing relevance, and its error-
less revelation of truth. Each of these principles holds immense importance, but let us give attention especially just now to the first and the last.
As you comprehend the nature of Scripture, you will find adequate reason
to accept biblical authority for your belief and practice.

Understanding the Bible's nature begins with comprehending the truth
of its divine origin. The Scriptures are "God-breathed" (2 Timothy 3:16).
The metaphor here is of the breath of God rendering a quiet, unseen
influence through the compulsive power of the Holy Spirit to produce
the unique revelation God intended. The meaning is that Scripture is
inherently inspired rather than that Scripture has an inspiring effect.

Paul used two terms for Scripture in 2 Timothy 3:15–16. He wrote
"holy Scriptures" or holy writings in verse 15. He was referring to the Old
Testament, which the Jewish people considered the authoritative Word of
God. In verse 16, "all scripture" (NIV) or "every scripture" translates
another word, "writing." This word may simply be a further reference to
the Old Testament. It might, however, also include other inspired writings such as New Testament sections. Peter spoke of Paul's epistles, which

The Bible in Action

Until 1954, the West Danis of Irian Jaya (Indonesia) had little contact with the outside world. Evangelistic work at first saw little response. Then, 2,000 Danis came to Christian faith, burned their traditional fetishes, and began to share the gospel with other Danis. On one day, in 1960, 8,000 Danis declared their faith in Christ and burned their fetishes.

Missionary James Sunda began meeting for prayer and Bible study with Dani leaders. One morning the Dani leaders said to Sunda, "We have been reading the Bible. It seems to teach that Christians should not kill others. Is that right?"

"Yes, that is right," answered Sunda.

"But," rejoined the Dani leaders, "Our way of life demands that we raise pigs, sacrifice them for our ancestors, hold a great feast, and then make war on the people in the next valley. That is what we have always believed and what we have always done. Now that we are Christians, should we not stop this?"

"That is correct," said Sunda. "What *are* you going to do?"

"We plan to have a big feast, invite our enemies, and while they are here, tell them we have become Christians and Christians do not kill others. We will burn one-half our weapons. They will know we cannot attack them but that if they attack us, we have enough weapons to defend ourselves."

What happened? The West Danis accepted a new authority. They changed from basing their beliefs (sacrificing to ancestors) and their practices (war) on their traditions to a new authority, the Bible.[15]

"contain some things that are hard to understand, which ignorant and unstable people distort, as they do the other Scriptures, to their own destruction" (2 Peter 3:16). So Peter placed Paul's epistles on the same level as the Old Testament.[6] "All Scripture" in verse 16 therefore likely includes both Old and New Testaments.

The biblical teachings as to the origin of Scripture follow a pattern. God revealed himself through his mighty acts—such as creation, exodus, incarnation, transfiguration, crucifixion, and resurrection. The Spirit of God moved writers to observe and comprehend what God was saying in the events. The same Spirit then guided these writers to write exactly the message God intended. God preserved these writings, and now the Spirit guides believers in understanding them. The Bible is, therefore, a revelation of divine origin, a revelation that is, as T. B. Maston said, "from God, of God, to man, through man."[7] The Bible thus constitutes the inspired, infallible Word of God.

The truth of its divine origin establishes the Bible as a unique authority for you—an authority that can be claimed by no other source. George W. Truett said, "Not traditions, nor customs, nor councils, nor confessions, nor ecclesiastical formularies, however venerable and pretentious, guide Baptists, but simply and solely the will of Christ as they find it revealed in the New Testament."[8]

The Bible also claims authority in your life because it represents ultimate truth. Scripture is the record of God's revelation of himself through inspired writers. Baptists, therefore, affirm the Scriptures as a "perfect treasure of divine instruction"[9] The Bible's authority in believers' lives

Some Notable Statements Concerning Biblical Authority:[16]

- "The ultimate source of authority is Jesus Christ the Lord, and every area of life is to be subject to his Lordship."
- "The Bible as the inspired revelation of God's will and way, made full and complete in the life and teachings of Christ, is our authoritative rule of faith and practice."
- "The Holy Spirit is God actively revealing himself and his will to people. He therefore interprets and confirms the voice of divine authority."

stems from the conviction that the Scriptures constitute "truth, without any mixture of error."[10]

Baptist statements of belief over the years have affirmed consistently that the Bible is the sole authority for faith and practice. "Sole authority" does not mean that Baptists find truth in no other source. Rather, it means that the Bible, when interpreted by the same Spirit who inspired it, is sufficient and able to guide believers to everything necessary for belief and behavior—for faith and practice. Christians accept other sources of truth only as they conform to the overall teachings of Scripture.

The assurance of the reliability, trustworthiness, and infallibility of Scripture assures believers that what the Bible teaches them to believe and practice will never be wrong. The totally inspired Bible never contradicts itself. No human statement of doctrine or the pronouncements of any Christian leader hold authority equal to the Bible.

The Bible will become authoritative in your life as you accept it as the Word of God leading without error to all matters of doctrine and behavior.

Flowing from Accurate Interpretation (2 Peter 1:19–21)

Scripture will become authoritative in your life as its teachings flow from accurate interpretation. In 2 Peter 1:19–21 the apostle was probably combating the gnostic heresy that regarded Christ as a lower manifestation of the highest deity. Peter declared that his being an eyewitness of the transfiguration gave a personal and dynamic insight to the majesty of Christ (2 Pet. 1:16–18).

In verse 19, "the word of the prophets made more certain," might mean that the prophetic witness had greater force than did Peter's eyewitness to the transfiguration. More likely, Peter's words mean that the transfiguration confirmed the messianic prophecies and made clear Christ's deity.[11]

The Bible Becomes
Authoritative for Any Christian:

- when that Christian comes to a personal experience with Christ through the Scriptures
- when that believer understands the nature of the Bible and accepts its divine origin and authority
- when that believer's understanding of the Bible flows from accurate interpretation of the Word
- when the believer understands and avails himself or herself of the living usefulness of Scripture
Allow the Spirit to make the Bible authoritative in your life!

Peter declared that the Scriptures did not come into being by the impulses or will of humans but rather by those "carried along" by the Spirit (1:21) so that they wrote the true and accurate Word of God. Peter did not argue for Scripture's inspiration; he assumed it.

To the conviction that the Holy Spirit directed the writing of Scripture, Peter added that the Spirit must also guide humans to understand and interpret the Word. The New International Version of verse 20 is, "no prophecy of Scripture came about by the prophet's own interpretation." Consider these other possible translations, too: "There is no prophetic teaching found in scripture that can be interpreted by man's unaided reason" (The Twentieth Century New Testament) and " . . . No prophetic scripture allows a man to interpret it by himself" (Moffatt). The Holy Spirit moved authors to write the Scriptures; the Spirit will also move people to understand and interpret it.

The Bible will assume a place of authority in your life only as you develop adequate methods of Bible study. When your interpretations flow from the Spirit who inspired the Scriptures, the teachings will assume a more powerful place in your life.

Providing Solid Guidance for Christian Living
(Psalm 119:97–112; Romans 15:4; 2 Timothy 3:14–17)

Scripture will become authoritative in your life as it provides solid and practical guidance for Christian living. Paul declares the Word "useful," that is, having potential to result in proper living (2 Tim. 3:16).

The Bible is useful in providing guidance for life. The guidance of the Scriptures assures believers that they will find and follow the will of God if they are faithful to biblical teachings (Psalm 119:104–105). Charles Wade has written, "We must always go to the Scriptures to find guidance and answers. . . . We must use the Bible as our plumb line, the standard by which we evaluate our own personal opinions and attitudes about a given issue."[12]

The Bible is useful in providing hope that leads to endurance. Paul, in Romans 15:4, indicated that Scripture was written "to teach us, so that through endurance and the encouragement of the Scriptures we might have hope."

The Bible is useful in providing conviction of sin. The words of Scripture bring to light the hidden sinfulness of our hearts and drive us to repentance (Hebrews 4:12–13). Few lessons are more advantageous than this.

The Uses of the Bible in the Believer's Life

- Guiding in Life and Thought
- Providing Hope that Leads to Endurance
- Instructing in the Fullest Meaning of Salvation
- Warning Against the Evils of Sin
- Producing Conviction of Sin
- Instructing in Religious and Ethical Thought
- Exposing Errors in Thought and Life (reproof)
- Restoring Doctrinal Truth and Ethical Behavior (correction)
- Training in Moral Living that Leads to Righteousness
- Equipping for Service

The Bible is useful in warning against sin. The psalmist considered the Word of God as of great benefit and power because in this Law the psalmist found wisdom, insight, and protection from sinful behavior (Ps. 119:97–102). God's Word guided the psalmist to hate sin and thereby avoid wrong paths (19:10–13; 119:104). For this reason, the psalmist had "hidden" (stored up and protected) the Word in his heart so that he would not sin against God (119:11).

The Bible is useful in leading to the full meaning of salvation. In 2 Timothy 3:14–17, the Apostle Paul declared that the Scriptures are able to "make you wise for salvation through faith in Christ Jesus" (3:15). The Bible leads believers in the dual dimensions of salvation—that is, how to be saved and how to live as a saved person.

The Bible is useful for teaching (instruction) in religious and ethical insight and for stimulating to deeper discipleship (2 Tim. 3:16). The presence of heresy in Timothy's day made sound doctrinal teaching imperative. Is this situation not also reflected today?

The Scriptures are useful for reproof ("rebuking"). Reproof exposes false teaching, reveals inadequate understanding, and unmasks false teachers. The term likely relates both to exposing false teachers and to exposing errors in our personal lives. "Scripture can show sinners their failures, clarify the point of the mistake, and lead them to a new sense of peace and wholeness."[13]

The Bible is useful for correction. This term suggests that the Bible helps Christians restore their doctrine and/or personal practice to conformity to the will of God. Correction involves a most positive factor in the use of Scripture.

Scripture also is useful in providing moral "training" that leads to righteous living. Paul employed this parental term for disciplining a child and developing his or her character. The term carries the idea of a system of discipline that leads to a divinely acceptable lifestyle.

The Bible is useful in equipping the people of God. As believers avail themselves of this profitable revelation, they will be "thoroughly equipped for every good work" (2 Tim. 3:17). "Thoroughly equipped" means *in fit shape or condition*. The result is that the worker is totally enabled to do whatever God calls on him or her to do and that this equipping is an abiding condition.[14] The Christian leader who accepts and lives by the authoritative Word of God will have the tools to deal with any task he or she might face.

The Scripture will assume authority in your life as you accept and act on its tremendous usefulness as a guide for Christian living.

The Bible, Our Sole and Sufficient Guide

For Baptists, the Bible is the sole and sufficient guide to all matters of belief and behavior—to faith and practice. Baptists, therefore, neither hold to a creed nor give total deference to the pronouncements of any leader. The authority for Baptists rests in Christ as Christ is revealed in the Scriptures. As you allow the Spirit to work in your life, you will affirm the Bible, and it will become more and more authoritative for you.

QUESTIONS

1. Are there areas of your life that are governed more by tradition, that is, what you have always believed or always been told, than by Scripture? List any such areas and write plans by which you might reverse this trend.

2. Of the ways described by which a believer might develop a deeper commitment to biblical authority, which do you think would be most profitable in your life?

3. Often we say Baptists accept the Scriptures as the sole authority for all matters of faith and practice. What problems do you see in the term, "sole"?

4. What do you think allows sincere, Bible-loving Christians to come to differing interpretations of Scripture? What should be done in such situations?

Notes

1. Walter Thomas Conner, *Christian Doctrine* (Nashville, Tennessee: Broadman Press, 1937), 42.
2. Russell H. Dilday, Jr., *The Doctrine of Biblical Authority* (Nashville: Convention Press, 1982), 20, italics in original.
3. Article 1, "The Baptist Faith and Message," 1963.
4. Herschel H. Hobbs, "The Authority of the Bible," Address at the Conference on Biblical Authority, Southeastern Baptist Theological Seminary, January 29–30, 1980, pages 5–7, and W. T. Conner, *Revelation and God* (Nashville: Broadman Press, 1936), 96.
5. Dilday, 29.
6. A. T. Robertson, *Word Pictures in the New Testament* (Nashville, Tennessee: Broadman Press, 1933), VI:179.
7. T. B. Maston, *Why Live the Christian Life?* (Nashville: Thomas Nelson, 1974), 47.
8. "Baptists and Religious Liberty," in *A Sourcebook for Baptist Heritage*, ed. H. Leon McBeth (Nashville: Broadman Press, 1990), 470. The full text of George W. Truett's sermon, "Baptists and Religious Liberty," can also be accessed on the internet at this address: http://www.bjcpa.org/pubs/fultruet.html
9. Article 1, "The Baptist Faith and Message," 1963.
10. Article 1, "The Baptist Faith and Message," 1963.
11. A. T. Robertson, VI:157.
12. Charles R. Wade, with Lee and Carol Bowman, *The Jesus Principle: Building Churches in the Likeness of Christ* (Arlington, TX: Clear Stream Publishing Inc., 1998), 169.
13. Thomas D. Lea, *1 & 2 Timothy*, The New American Commentary (Nashville: Broadman Press, 1992), 237.
14. Lea, 237.
15. See James Sunda, *Church Growth in West New Guinea* (Lucknow, India: Lucknow Publishing House, 1963), 22–45; Donald A. McGavran, *Understanding Church Growth*, 3d ed. (Grand Rapids: Eerdmans, 1990), 128, 241, 256–57.
16. From "Baptist Ideals" a statement prepared for the 1964 celebration of the one hundred and fiftieth anniversary of the organization of the first Baptist national organization in America. Prepared by a committee chaired by Ralph A Herring. Contained in Walter B. Shurden, *The Baptist Identity: Four Fragile Freedoms* (Macon, Georgia: Smyth & Helwys Publishing,1993), 103–104.

The Autonomy of the Local Congregation of Believers

BACKGROUND SCRIPTURES

Matthew 18:15–20; Acts 6:3–6; 13:1–3; 14:23,27; 15:1–30; 16:5; 20:28; 1 Corinthians 1:2; 5:1–5; Revelation 2—3

FOCAL TEXTS

Matthew 18:15–20; Acts 6:3–6; 13:1–3; 1 Corinthians 5:1–5

MAIN IDEA

"Each local church is self-governing and independent in the management of its affairs."[1]

STUDY AIM

To explain why Baptists believe that each local church is autonomous and identify implications of this idea

QUICK READ

Members of a local Baptist church have the responsibility and privilege of making the decisions that chart the church's course. No external authority can tell a Baptist church what to do.

When the controversy in the Southern Baptist Convention erupted at the 1979 Houston meeting, confused reporters needed lots of help. They didn't understand how decisions made in Houston held no power over the local church to make changes. Glenn Hilburn, a friend of mine and a professor of church history at Baylor University, held briefings to explain the structure of Baptist churches, associations, and the national organization to the non-Baptist reporters. The media representatives still shook their heads and murmured. They couldn't comprehend a people whose national organization did not dictate the actions of the local church. Sometimes I'll have a non-Baptist in my Baptist History class, and they, like the reporters, struggle with how Baptists operate.

Baptists structure their churches as congregations in which the members make the decisions and choose to cooperate with other like-minded churches. This polity (structure) makes sense when you look at the Baptist doctrines we've studied. Salvation by grace, soul competency, priesthood of the believers, symbolic ordinances—it makes sense that Baptist church structure reflects the basic belief in the individual responsibility of a believer to work for the kingdom of God, share the gospel, and join a community of faith for nurture and growth. Of course the individual believer would have a voice in the governance of the church! We call this way of doing a church's work the autonomy of the local church. "Autonomy" comes from the Greek words *autos* and *nomos*, meaning "self" and "law." An autonomous church rules itself.

Many Christian denominations structure their churches and the relationships between congregations differently than Baptists do. Each type of church structure rests on a certain interpretation of biblical passages. When Baptists developed in the early 1600s and searched Scripture for their model of church polity, they understood the overall sense of Scripture to support a congregational model as we have today. Acts 6:3–6 taught them that churches choose their own leaders. Matthew 18:15–20 and 1 Corinthians 5:1–5 taught them that churches decide how to discipline members. And Acts 13:1–3 taught them that local churches choose people for ministry as led by the Holy Spirit.

Matthew 18:15-20 (NRSV)

¹⁵"If another member of the church sins against you, go and point out the fault when the two of you are alone. If the member listens to you, you have regained that one. ¹⁶But if you are not listened to, take one or two others along with you, so that every word may be confirmed by the evidence of two or three witnesses. ¹⁷If the member refuses to listen to them, tell it to the church; and if the offender refuses to listen even to the church, let such a one be to you as a Gentile and a tax collector. ¹⁸Truly I tell you, whatever you bind on earth will be bound in heaven, and whatever you loose on earth will be loosed in heaven. ¹⁹Again, truly I tell you, if two of you agree on earth about anything you ask, it will be done for you by my Father in heaven. ²⁰For where two or three are gathered in my name, I am there among them."

Acts 6:3-6

³Therefore, friends, select from among yourselves seven men of good standing, full of the Spirit and of wisdom, whom we may appoint to this task, ⁴while we, for our part, will devote ourselves to prayer and to serving the word." ⁵What they said pleased the whole community, and they chose Stephen, a man full of faith and the Holy Spirit, together with Philip, Prochorus, Nicanor, Timon, Parmenas, and Nicolaus, a proselyte of Antioch. ⁶They had these men stand before the apostles, who prayed and laid their hands on them.

Acts 13:1-3

¹Now in the church at Antioch there were prophets and teachers: Barnabas, Simeon who was called Niger, Lucius of Cyrene, Manaen a member of the court of Herod the ruler, and Saul. ²While they were worshiping the Lord and fasting, the Holy Spirit said, "Set apart for me Barnabas and Saul for the work to which I have called them." ³Then after fasting and praying they laid their hands on them and sent them off.

1 Corinthians 5:1–5

¹It is actually reported that there is sexual immorality among you, and of a kind that is not found even among pagans; for a man is living with his father's wife. ²And you are arrogant! Should you not rather have mourned, so that he who has done this would have been removed from among you?

³For though absent in body, I am present in spirit; and as if present I have already pronounced judgment ⁴in the name of the Lord Jesus on the man who has done such a thing. When you are assembled, and my spirit is present with the power of our Lord Jesus, ⁵you are to hand this man over to Satan for the destruction of the flesh, so that his spirit may be saved in the day of the Lord.

God Is Present . . . (Acts 6:3–6)

God is present where two or three are gathered in the Lord's name (Matthew 18:20). So, wherever believers gather, they have the leadership of the Holy Spirit as a community of faith. They thus can make all the decisions necessary as a congregation. As individuals, each person carries the responsibility to live for God, to interpret Scripture, and to be Christ in the world. But as a community of faith, God's presence sharpens those responsibilities and focuses them for the good of the church.

In Acts 6:3–6, God focused the concept of service for the Jerusalem church. The apostles spent their time in worship and teaching the new Christians. They didn't have time to take care of the needy of the congregation. Under Jewish law, God required believers to take special care of widows and orphans. The Greek-speaking widows in the Jerusalem church felt neglected by the leaders. The church solved the problem by choosing from the congregation seven people to act as servants in distributing food and other necessities to the needy. For our study this week, the important point is that the people chose the servants. Peter and the other apostles did not say, "You, you, and you." Rather, they relied on the Holy Spirit working in the average church member to choose wisely.

The folks in the congregation looked for Spirit-filled and God-directed believers who could do the job. The members worked from their knowledge of each other and what the job required. Once the congregation chose the seven servants, the apostles set the men aside for special duties in a public ceremony. The public ceremony did not give the men special power. The laying on of hands simply indicated to the assembly that the servants accepted their new responsibilities and that the church made a covenant with them to help with the work. The members of the congregation chose wisely, for the servants did the job and did it well.

In Acts 6:3–6, the autonomy of the local church shines through. People perceived a need. The congregation, under the leadership of the Holy Spirit, determined a way to meet the need. The members chose people to do the actual work. No one told the congregation what they must do. No one ordered the selection of certain people. No one said, "If you don't do it this way, you aren't a true believer."

For Baptists, the Bible affirms that the local church is responsible for its own business, both spiritual and practical. The congregation may choose to cooperate with others, as in an association or convention, but "other groups or churches cannot take away the decision-making responsibilities of the local congregation."[2] God is present where two or three are gathered, and those two or three must make their own decisions under God's leadership.

When Decisions Have to Be Made . . .
(Matthew 18:15–20; 1 Corinthians 5:1–5)

When I teach Church History or Baptist History and come to the lecture on church discipline, the topic always creates discomfort. No one wants to be seen as judgmental or fanatical. Saying to fellow church members that they need to mend their ways requires special care. Thankfully, this lesson centers on the autonomy of the local church. So I don't have to deal specifically with the issue of church discipline. But we will focus on these passages as they make the point that the local church, and not some external agency or group, chooses what shall and shall not require discipline.

The New Testament teaches that the local church has responsibility for taking care of both practical and spiritual matters in its midst. Both Matthew 18:15–20 and 1 Corinthians 5:1–5 clearly note that the local folks must make decisions for the good of the congregation as well as the good of individual members. In some denominations, discipline is ordered by a hierarchy outside the local church. For Baptists, discipline remains within the control of the local congregation. Furthermore, discipline is a congregational decision, not the decision of one or two people.

These passages assert that God's presence with a group of believers establishes the necessary power for making decisions. Matthew 18 does not say you must wait until an outside authority gives an order before your congregation can act. In 1 Corinthians 5, Paul urged the community of faith to remove an immoral member. Paul, however, also recognized that the action must result from the leadership of God. Central to Baptist thought lies the notion that the corporate consciousness of Christ comes through when a congregation meets to make a decision. Paul's concerns, aired in a meeting and commented on, might galvanize the Corinthian church to take action. Still, Paul could only suggest action. The final decision rested with the folks in Corinth and how they perceived God's leadership.

From the days of the New Testament, local churches have cooperated with one another to accomplish greater good. In Romans 16:1–2, we learn that churches accepted members from other congregations. First Corinthians 16:1–4 shows that churches pooled their resources in a good cause. And the existence of the New Testament itself proves that churches shared letters and information among themselves for the good of all (Colossians 4:16–17).[3] While acting as autonomous churches, congregations still cooperated in many endeavors.

For modern Baptists, the issue becomes complicated because autonomous local churches have chosen to relate to one another and cooperate to accomplish tasks that single congregations could not. We relate to other Baptist churches in our geographical area through the local association and the state convention. Each group we relate to has the right and responsibility to set standards for the relationship. We as a church have a voice in establishing those standards. If for some reason we deviate from the standards set, then the association or convention has the authority to "dis-fellowship" us, to withdraw cooperation, and we must go on our way. Each level of relationship makes its own decisions based on what the members believe to be right.

For example, one Baptist association chose to welcome a woman as pastor of one of the churches. Affirming the local congregation members' right to choose their own pastor, the association treated and worked with her church as it had for decades. Another association nearby chose to "dis-fellowship" a church for calling a woman minister. For the members of that association, the standard of who could be a church minister did

Setting People Apart for Service

In the New Testament, a church would set people apart in public ceremonies for special tasks, as with the Antioch congregation laying hands on Paul and Barnabas (Acts 13:1–3). Such a ceremony was not a requirement to be met before becoming a minister. The Bible emphasizes that the lives of the people chosen for special work, whether Phoebe of Cenchreae (Romans 16:1), Philip of Samaria (Acts 6:5), or Epaphroditus of Philippi (Philippians 2:25), bore testimony to God's presence. The Holy Spirit led and reinforced the congregation's decision.

not include women. Thus that association excluded the congregation in question. For our purposes in this lesson, I must affirm both decisions. Both decisions recognized that the local church must make its own choices, but also that those choices carry consequences. However I feel personally about the "right" or "wrong" of women in ministry—and as a woman minister in the teaching profession, I have strong opinions!—both associations acted within mainstream Baptist doctrine because neither dictated to the local church who must be their pastor.

Baptists historically have affirmed local church autonomy, but we also have asserted cooperation for missions, evangelism, and so forth. Many churches working together accomplish more than one church. In 1814 churches across America joined together to support Anne Hazeltine and Adoniram Judson as missionaries by forming the Baptist General Missionary Convention. When these churches joined together, they agreed to work together for missions. Note that as individual churches they differed greatly! They worshiped in different ways. They had different concepts of who should be church leaders. They felt differently about including people of other races in their memberships. They had different concepts of the atonement and the work of the Holy Spirit. However, they all agreed that God wanted them to support and do missions. So they put aside their differences, differences they saw as less important than missions. They focused on the all-important task of missions.

Your Spiritual Gifts

Knowing your spiritual gifts will help you decide in which areas of church service to engage. Determine your gifts by talking with Christian friends who know you well, thinking about what you like to do and do well in the church, and praying for God to show you what gifts the Spirit has placed in your life. Read 1 Corinthians 12:4–11 and Ephesians 4:11–13 to see whether one or more of those gifts fits you.

Mainstream Baptists have worked to accept diversity while maintaining cooperation among congregations. In 1845, the Southern Baptist Convention split from the General Missionary Convention because the difference in the Northern and Southern views of slavery caused too much trouble.

In recent years, splits have occurred among Baptists because a church's concept of Scripture or of ministry or of missions or of ministerial authority differed too much from what a group accepted as true. A tough question facing twenty-first-century Baptists is, "How much difference is too much?" In the past, Baptists have accepted a great deal of difference and still cooperated. Today, mainstream Baptists still accept differences and cooperate. How much difference is "too much"? And who answers that question for you?

Concerning the Work of the Kingdom . . . (Acts 13:1–3)

I grew up attending Sunbeams, GAs, and YWAs. I served as a Journeyman missionary. Missions was, is, and always will be important to me. So, with great pleasure, I turn our attention to the concept of local church autonomy as it worked out in missions in the first century.

The story should be familiar to you. Barnabas, the Son of Encouragement, traveled to Antioch of Syria because the Jerusalem church heard that a Christian congregation had taken root there and was growing rapidly. Barnabas found the young congregation thriving and on target with their understanding of the gospel. Calling in Paul to help teach and nurture the young believers, the two men worked with the church for more than a year (Acts 11:19–30).

As the congregation was worshiping and fasting, the Holy Spirit led the congregation to "set apart" these two leaders "for the work to which I have called them" (13:2). In Judaism and early Christianity, a person fasted to emphasize the importance of a serious request. A person also fasted to focus on prayer and the will of God. So, because the people in Antioch wanted to know God's will, and they were serious about the effort, the Holy Spirit led the congregation to set aside Barnabas and Paul for special work. The Antioch folks became the first missionary sending organization! And Paul and Barnabas, the first full-fledged missionaries!

The local church made the choice under God's leadership. The local congregation responded to the prompting of the Holy Spirit in choosing the ones to be sent. The local church thus is seen to be the basic organizational building block of Baptist missionary efforts.

Over the years, the way churches did missions changed. In 1792, British Baptists formed the Baptist Missionary Society to send William and Dorothy Carey, and others, to India to preach the gospel. In 1814, the General Missionary Convention was formed in America to support Anne Hazeltine and Adoniram Judson's work in Burma. In 1845, when Southern Baptists split from the General Convention, the messengers to the formation convention established the Foreign Mission Board and the Domestic Mission Board before anything else. Why the move away from the Antioch model of an individual church sending missionaries?

The basic answer is that Baptists are a practical people. They figured out that by pooling funds, they could send more missionaries, and equip them better, than a single church could. Because missions carried such importance, most Baptist churches modified their concern for absolute local autonomy to participate in the larger missions effort. However, some folks did not believe the Bible authorized any agency beyond the local church. Thus they refused to be part of missionary societies or conventions. These congregations, known as Anti-Mission Baptists, acted true to their Baptist heritage of local church decision-making. They chose not to join associations or conventions. If one of these churches engaged in missions or evangelism, it pursued the activity without help from others.

For the Anti-Mission Baptists, the cooperating Baptists moved too far from a certain interpretation of Scripture, and so fellowship was broken. For the cooperating Baptists, the Anti-Mission folks interpreted the Bible too narrowly. The command to preach the gospel to the world held more importance than an interpretation condemning missionary organizations beyond the local church. Both groups took seriously the autonomy of the local church, but they understood that autonomy differently when they related it to the Great Commission.

A Current Concern

A modern development threatening the Baptist doctrine of the autonomy of the local church is the adoption by some congregations of the business model with a CEO running the operation. If the pastor functions as a CEO, and the paid ministerial staff work for the pastor, what role does the congregational member have? When the CEO makes all the decisions and simply informs the congregation, what remains for the member to do besides supply money? This increasingly popular organizational model is not Baptist, and it undercuts the rights and privileges of individual members of the congregation. Ministers, in Baptist life, are not "rulers." They are "servants." Remember, ultimately we are all priests.

QUESTIONS

1. What do you think of the CEO model for a pastor? Why might folks prefer that model to the historical Baptist model?

2. How seriously do you take your responsibilities as a church member?

3. Whose responsibility is the running of the church? the mission of the church? the finances of the church?

Notes

1. Walter Thomas Conner, *Christian Doctrine* (Nashville, Tennessee: Broadman Press, 1937), 266.
2. Rosalie Beck, "The Church is Free to Make Its Own Decisions under the Lordship of Christ," in *Defining Baptist Convictions for the Twenty-First Century*, ed. Charles W. Deweese (Franklin, Tennessee: Providence House Publishers, 1996), 131.
3. H. Leon McBeth, "Autonomy and Cooperation," in the *Foundations of Baptist Heritage Series* (Nashville, Tennessee: The Historical Commission of the Southern Baptist Convention, 1989), 1.

Believer's Baptism and Church Membership

BACKGROUND SCRIPTURES

Matthew 28:19–20; Mark 1:9–11; Luke 3:21–22; John 3:23; Acts 2:14–47; 5:11–14; 8:26–39; 16:11–15, 25–34; Romans 1:7; 6:3–5; 1 Corinthians 1:2; 3:16; Colossians 2:12

FOCAL TEXTS

Acts 8:26–38; 16:11–15, 25–34

MAIN IDEA

" . . . The only person properly qualified for baptism is one who has heard the gospel, accepted its message, and believed in Christ as . . . Savior."[1] "Only those should be received into church membership who give credible evidence that they have received Christ as Savior and Lord."[2]

STUDY AIM

To state the meaning of believer's baptism and why it is important

QUICK READ

Baptism, the immersion of a believer in water in the name of the Holy Trinity, symbolizes the total salvation experience, testifies of the believer's commitment to Jesus, and provides access to church membership.

The baptismal service had been announced, the baptismal pool had been prepared, and the two teenage women candidates were present and ready. What was more, the unsaved father of one of the young women together with three unsaved friends of both were present. It promised to be a significant worship experience and a tremendous witnessing opportunity.

As is too often the case, a problem also arose. For reasons still undetermined, the water in the baptismal pool was near the boiling point. Deacons said we would just have to postpone the service. I told them that the unsaved father and the unsaved friends were present and that we must have the baptismal service that morning. We could wait until the end of the morning rather than early in the service, but we had to do it that morning.

"What will we do?" asked the deacons.

"I don't know," I answered. "I must begin the service. You are the deacons. You will work it out."

We heard strange noises from the baptistery during the service. At the time for the baptismal service, the minister of youth proceeded to baptize both young women—one by her baptism testifying to her own father and both of them to their friends.

What had happened to make the baptismal pool usable? During the service, the deacons had purchased fifty-two bags of ice and put them into it. The water was then cool enough for the service to proceed.

What was the big deal? Why not postpone the service? The young women were believers; their salvation did not depend on their baptism. The young women needed in obedience to their Lord to follow him in baptism, but that could wait a week. The baptism had to be Scriptural; immersion was necessary. The witness of baptism was imperative, though, especially in view of the presence of the unsaved father and their unsaved friends. The church was prepared to receive the two into membership. Baptism that day was important!

What actually is baptism and why is it important in the Christian life? This lesson seeks to guide you to understand fully, accept personally, and explain adequately the biblical meaning of baptism—its religious significance and its eternal importance.

Acts 8:26–38 (NIV)

26Now an angel of the Lord said to Philip, "Go south to the road—the desert road—that goes down from Jerusalem to Gaza." 27So he started out, and on his way he met an Ethiopian eunuch, an important official in charge of all the treasury of Candace, queen of the Ethiopians. This man had gone to Jerusalem to worship, 28and on his way home was sitting in his chariot reading the book of Isaiah the prophet. 29The Spirit told Philip, "Go to that chariot and stay near it."

30Then Philip ran up to the chariot and heard the man reading Isaiah the prophet. "Do you understand what you are reading?" Philip asked.

31"How can I," he said, "unless someone explains it to me?" So he invited Philip to come up and sit with him.

32 The eunuch was reading this passage of Scripture:

"He was led like a sheep to the slaughter,
and as a lamb before the shearer is silent,
so he did not open his mouth.
33 In his humiliation he was deprived of justice.
Who can speak of his descendants?
For his life was taken from the earth."

34The eunuch asked Philip, "Tell me, please, who is the prophet talking about, himself or someone else?" 35Then Philip began with that very passage of Scripture and told him the good news about Jesus.

36As they traveled along the road, they came to some water and the eunuch said, "Look, here is water. Why shouldn't I be baptized?" 38And he gave orders to stop the chariot. Then both Philip and the eunuch went down into the water and Philip baptized him.

The Meaning of Baptism
(Acts 8:26–38; 16:11–15, 25–34)

What is the biblical meaning of baptism? We can capsule this meaning by considering two significant words—*believer* and *symbolic*. Biblical teachings restrict baptism to people who have repented of their sins, accepted Christ as Savior, and determined to follow him as Lord. The

Acts 16:11–15, 25–34

[11]From Troas we put out to sea and sailed straight for Samothrace, and the next day on to Neapolis. [12]From there we traveled to Philippi, a Roman colony and the leading city of that district of Macedonia. And we stayed there several days.

[13]On the Sabbath we went outside the city gate to the river, where we expected to find a place of prayer. We sat down and began to speak to the women who had gathered there. [14]One of those listening was a woman named Lydia, a dealer in purple cloth from the city of Thyatira, who was a worshiper of God. The Lord opened her heart to respond to Paul's message. [15]When she and the members of her household were baptized, she invited us to her home. "If you consider me a believer in the Lord," she said, "come and stay at my house." And she persuaded us.

• •

[25]About midnight Paul and Silas were praying and singing hymns to God, and the other prisoners were listening to them. [26]Suddenly there was such a violent earthquake that the foundations of the prison were shaken. At once all the prison doors flew open, and everybody's chains came loose. [27]The jailer woke up, and when he saw the prison doors open, he drew his sword and was about to kill himself because he thought the prisoners had escaped. [28]But Paul shouted, "Don't harm yourself! We are all here!"

[29]The jailer called for lights, rushed in and fell trembling before Paul and Silas. [30]He then brought them out and asked, "Sirs, what must I do to be saved?"

[31]They replied, "Believe in the Lord Jesus, and you will be saved—you and your household." [32]Then they spoke the word of the Lord to him and to all the others in his house. [33]At that hour of the night the jailer took them and washed their wounds; then immediately he and all his family were baptized. [34]The jailer brought them into his house and set a meal before them; he was filled with joy because he had come to believe in God—he and his whole family.

passages for study present accounts of salvation experiences in the New Testament—each of which point to salvation coming before baptism.

On the day of Pentecost a miraculous event empowered the gathered disciples to proclaim the gospel in different languages so that peoples from many different lands could understand it in their most familiar tongues (Acts 2:1–13). Peter proclaimed God's message, explaining that the observed event had been foretold by the prophet Joel and that God would bring salvation to all who accepted the message (2:14–36). After hearing Peter's witness, the people cried, "What shall we do?" (2:37). Peter's answer was, "'Repent and be baptized, every one of you, in the name of Jesus Christ for the forgiveness of your sins. And you will receive the gift of the Holy Spirit'" (2:38).

Some confusion exists concerning this verse. Some have understood it to teach baptism as essential for salvation rather than a testimony of salvation. Understanding the verse hinges on the word, "for," which may be translated *for, unto, on the basis of, with respect to,* or even *as a result of.*[3] The word is used in Matthew 12:41 and Luke 11:32 with reference to the preaching of Jonah, saying that the people in Nineveh repented "at" the preaching of Jonah. Clearly, the meaning is not that they repented so that Jonah could preach but as a result of the preaching. Interpreting Acts 2:38 as meaning "repent and be baptized" *as a result of* or *on the basis of* the forgiveness of sins is linguistically sound and conforms to the broad teachings of the New Testament on the subjects of salvation and baptism.

Acts 8:26–38. The same teaching springs from the account of the deacon Philip and the treasury official from the land of Ethiopia (Acts 8:26–38). That the Ethiopian had been in Jerusalem for worship suggests he may well have been a proselyte or at least a God-fearer. (The term *God-fearer* refers to a person who was not a full-fledged Jew but who nevertheless worshiped the God of Israel.) The Ethiopian was reading Isaiah 53:7. He could not understand it, however, until Philip explained the Isaiah text and also told him the good news about Jesus (Acts 8:35).

Upon hearing the witness concerning Jesus, the Ethiopian cried out (8:36), "'Look, here is water, Why shouldn't I be baptized?'" The evangelist and the new believer descended from the chariot and went down into the water. Philip baptized the new convert (Acts 8:38). Verse 37, as it appears in the King James Version, is not adequately supported by the earlier manuscripts and is not in Lukan style. Therefore, most authorities consider the verse a later addition and not a part of the original, inspired text. Even without verse 37, the most likely understanding is that baptism follows and pictures salvation.

Acts 16:11–15. Two events in Acts 16, the conversion and baptism of Lydia and the jailer, took place in the city of Philippi. These events underline the proper sequence—salvation then baptism (16:11–15,25–34). Paul and his group had sailed from Troas, in the Roman province of Asia, to the island of Samothrace, and from there to Neapolis, the port city. Neapolis was about ten miles from Philippi in Macedonia, which was located in the area of modern-day Greece.

No record exists of Paul entering a synagogue in Philippi. Since ten adult men were required for establishing a synagogue, one may not have existed. Paul and his group went on the Sabbath to a place on the river, thinking a Jewish place of worship existed there. The apostle found there a group of worshiping women, including Lydia. She came from the city of Thyatira in the Roman province of Asia. Thyatira was well-known for its purple cloth. Lydia may have dealt in this cloth. More importantly, she was a "worshiper of God," perhaps already a proselyte (16:14). "The Lord opened her heart" and brought her to salvation (16:14). After her salvation, Lydia and her "household"—that is, family, slaves, and other dependents—were baptized (16:15). Clearly, salvation came first and then baptism.

Acts 16:25–34. The experience of the jailer in Philippi reinforces this teaching. After Paul cast the evil spirit from the slave girl and ruined the moneymaking scheme of some citizens of Philippi, these businessmen had Paul and Silas jailed (see Acts 16:16–24). Their prayers and hymns testified to their faith. The earthquake at midnight opened the doors and unlocked the shackles that held them. Thinking the prisoners had escaped, the jailer was in the process of falling on his sword when Paul stopped him. So impressed was the jailer that he called for the apostles and asked (16:29), "'What must I do to be saved?'" After salvation, he and his family were baptized. Once again, the meaning of baptism demands that saving faith precede it.

Ancient Baptismal Practices

Christianity was not the only religion to practice baptism in biblical times. Several different religious groups used baptism as a ritual relating to the removal of guilt and the beginning of a new life. Some of the mystery religions (called "mystery" religions because they used secret rites and methods) used baptism at times, even in blood. Around the time of Jesus, the Jews began using baptism for Gentile converts to Judaism.

The baptism of John the Baptist was similar to but different from that which early Christians used. John's baptism was one of repentance, calling people back to faithfulness and commitment to the law of God (Matt. 3:5–12; Luke 3:3). The baptism of John related to moral and ethical purification. Second, John's baptism looked forward to the coming of Messiah (Matt. 3:2; Mark 1:7–8).

Jesus followed John's baptism, thus showing the Lord's identification with the religious concerns of John and with sinful humanity (Matt 3:15; 2 Cor. 5:21). The Lord adapted baptism for his movement, commanding his followers to baptize those who became followers. Paul's understanding was that one was baptized into Christ, referring to relationship to Christ.

Baptism in the New Testament demonstrates a rich symbolism and a vital purpose. It became the first public act that identified believers with the death and resurrection of Christ. Baptism symbolized the inclusion of a person into the saving mission of Jesus.

Baptism's meaning begins with the fact that only a believer, a saved person, should be baptized. This biblical truth rules out baptizing babies or others who cannot personally respond to Jesus in faith. The truth also denies any practice of being baptized for others—such as people who have already died. Only a person saved by faith in Jesus Christ can be properly baptized.

A second significant word, symbolic, also describes the meaning of baptism. Baptists regard baptism and the Lord's Supper as purely, totally, and only symbolic, with no power to save. Baptism, like the Lord's Supper, contains no magical meaning or power. Although meaningful religious rituals, these ordinances do not confer divine power or favor. The concept that some divine power resides in religious forms is called sacramentalism, and Baptists strongly resist any tendency toward such belief.

The Apostle Paul insisted that people are saved by grace through faith and not by works (Romans 3:21–31; Ephesians 2:8–10). The works to which he denied any saving power were religious rituals—such as were practiced in Jewish ceremonial law. Baptism symbolizes and pictures salvation. It does not give salvation; it is not required for salvation; and its absence does not withhold salvation.

For Baptists, Baptism Is:

- a symbolic act whereby a believer is immersed in water to picture salvation, new life, and commitment to Christ
- a public act of obedience by a believer
- a beautiful symbol of the totality of Christ's saving work in the believer
- a picture of the believer's death to sin and an expression of the believer's intention to walk in Christ's way
- an affirmation of the believer's faith in Christ's promised return
- an opening for the believer's entrance into church membership
- a testimony of the believer's trust in Christ

Baptism symbolizes the total Christian experience. The one accepting baptism expresses his or her confession of faith in Christ, pictures in the act of baptism his or her burial or death to sin, and acknowledges his or her confidence in a resurrection to new life. The act of being baptized also expresses the believer's vital spiritual relationship with Christ. Only a saved person can join such a celebration (see Rom. 6:3–5). W. R. White wrote, "Baptists do not believe that baptism is essential to salvation, but they do believe that salvation is essential to baptism."[4]

The Mode of Baptism

How should baptism be practiced or administered? Is immersion in water really important or will some other mode equally express the meaning of baptism?

The basic meaning of the word *baptize* shows that Scriptural baptism requires immersion. Every lexicon (dictionary) of the Greek language defines the word *baptize* in terms such as dipping, submerging, immersing, or cleansing by submerging. The same teaching appears in the Septuagint (the Greek translation of the Old Testament) where Naaman "dipped himself in the Jordan" (2 Kings 5:14). The basic meaning of the word *baptize* is beyond dispute.

Immersion represents the New Testament mode for baptism. Only years after the apostolic period did another way of baptizing—by sprinkling or pouring—arise. The modification in mode of baptism arose out of a change in its meaning and significance—primarily as some groups came to consider baptism essential to salvation. The New Testament mode of baptism clearly is immersion in water.

Descriptions of baptism in biblical accounts support the teaching of immersion as the Scriptural mode of baptism. John was baptizing at Aenon, near Salim, "because there was plenty of water" (John 3:23). After Jesus' baptism, he "was coming up out of the water" (Mark 1:9–11).

The man from Ethiopia and Philip went down to the water and "came up out of the water" (Acts 8:39). These and other verses strongly suggest immersion as the way baptism was done.

The very symbolism of the act requires immersion to express fully the meaning. Paul wrote, "having been buried with him in baptism, and raised with him through your faith in the power of God, who raised him from the dead" (Col. 2:12, see also Rom. 6:3–5). Only immersion completely symbolizes the believer's experience—picturing the believer's dying to sin, being raised to walk in newness of life, and expecting the Second Coming.

The Mandate for Baptism

Why is baptism important? If it does not give salvation and one can be saved without it, why go to the trouble of doing it? Three thoughts—*obedience, ordinance,* and *church membership*—clarify the mandate for baptism.

Baptism is an act of obedience to Christ. In the Great Commission (Matthew 28:19–20), Jesus instructed his followers to "make disciples" of all peoples in the world. One part of the process of making disciples involved " baptizing them" in the name of the Holy Trinity. Baptism expresses obedience on the part of the believer and on the part of the church.

Baptists describe baptism with the term *ordinance*, meaning a practice that is commanded, decreed, mandated, or instructed by the Lord. Through history, Baptists have avoided the term *sacrament* because of the entanglement of this term with ritual acts that confer or give grace or forgiveness. The term sacrament may have slipped into Christian usage since the Latin word *sacramentum* signified the oath a Roman soldier took upon becoming a member of the legions. The ordinances may have been seen as the believer's declaration of his or her allegiance to Christ.[5] But

Ethiopia

In biblical times, the designation of the nation Ethiopia was somewhat vague, but most likely the nation corresponds to the area of modern Nubia. The king in Ethiopia was thought to be too sacred a person to discharge secular business. So these functions were carried out by the queen mother, who generally bore the dynastic title, Candace.

An angel of the Lord guided Philip to a road in the desert that ran southwest from Jerusalem to Gaza, a Phoenician city about sixty miles from Jerusalem. On that road, Philip contacted the court official.

the sense of sacrament as a dispenser or giver of grace and salvation has never been accepted by Baptists.

Baptists acknowledge only two ordinances—baptism and the Lord's Supper. Other rituals, such as foot washing (John 13:1–17), might very well be moving and deeply spiritual worship services. A service of foot washing is not, however, commanded by the Lord for his churches as are baptism and the Lord's Supper.

Church membership constitutes the third idea that describes the mandate for baptism. As the 1963 Baptist Faith and Message stated, "Being a church ordinance, it is prerequisite to the privileges of church membership and to the Lord's Supper."[6] Baptism is not required for entrance into the Kingdom of God. It does, however, form the "door" to the local church and is necessary for membership in the local church.

Baptism is important; it constitutes a mandate from the Lord and a need in the Christian life. Its importance does not stem from any sense that the ritual brings or gives salvation, however. Baptism's importance consists of (1) demonstrating a believer's obedience to Christ; (2) offering a testimony of a believer's trust in Christ, (3) and providing the believer a means to become a part of the local church.

Baptism—A Personal Experience

The students at our Indonesian Baptist Theological Seminary and I had started a church in the central Java town of Salatiga. The church had grown under the leadership of a seminary student. He came to me one day and announced that twelve people were to be baptized at Salatiga the next Sunday.

"Praise God," I said.

Then came the student's question, "Will you come and baptize them?"

"Why don't you baptize them," I returned. "You are the pastor; you won them to Christ!"

"I can't do it," said the student. "I'm not ordained."

"What's that got to do with it?" I asked.

"Well," he said, "I'm *malu* [shy or embarrassed]."

"Ok," I answered. "If your church asks me I will come and baptize them if you will agree that the next time you will do it."

Then he told me that the baptismal service would be held in the public swimming pool. My western mind thought, public swimming pool, Sunday, closed. When we reached the swimming pool Sunday afternoon, it was filled with swimmers. The pastor walked around the pool, calling, "Everyone out, we are having baptism." The swimmers didn't know what baptism was, but they got out and sat so quietly that I preached on the meaning of baptism.

After the baptism, walking back to the church building, I remarked to the church members that the service was exactly what baptism is. These twelve believers had given a public, open, courageous testimony of their faith in Christ—and everyone could witness it!

Then I did a no-no. I had to go out of the country and left money with the leaders of the church to build a baptistery at the church building. When I returned, there was the baptistery—right outside the building, with no roof or walls. They had made a window in the building so people inside could look out and see the baptistery.

Patiently, I asked why they had built the baptistery outside the building. "Well," they said, "You told us that baptism means an open, public, courageous testimony of faith in Christ. Had we put the baptistery inside the building the only ones who could witness it would be church members inside the building. This way, everyone up on the road can see the baptisms and receive the testimonies of those being baptized."

The members in Salatiga were correct! That is exactly what baptism is—an open, public, courageous testimony of one's placing one's faith in Christ, leaving the old life, and being made alive to new life. Baptism holds great importance both to Christians and the churches into which they are gathered.

QUESTIONS

1. How would you answer a person who says that baptism actually is not important to a Christian or to churches and the way it is done is even less important?

2. Do you think there is a danger is baptizing a person very soon after that person expresses faith in Christ? Is there a danger in waiting too long?

3. Why is baptism important both to Christians and to churches?

4. A wealthy woman came to the pastor of a church and said, "It is time I was baptized. I want you, pastor, to baptize me in a private ceremony with only my husband present. I think I will feel much better once I have been baptized." What unbiblical understandings do you see in this story (a true event, by the way)?

Notes

1. Walter Thomas Conner, *Christian Doctrine* (Nashville, Tennessee: Broadman Press, 1937), 282.
2. Conner, *Christian Doctrine*, 260.
3. Herschel H. Hobbs, *The Baptist Faith and Message* (Nashville: Convention Press, 1971), 86.
4. W. R. White, *Baptist Distinctives* (Nashville: Convention Press, 1956), 31–32.
5. H. E. Dana, *A Manual of Ecclesiology*, 2d ed. (Kansas City, Kansas: Central Seminary Press, 1944), 281.
6. Article 7, "The Baptist Faith and Message," 1963.

Congregational Church Government

BACKGROUND SCRIPTURES

Matthew 18:15–20; Acts 2:41–42,47; 5:11–14; 6:1–6; 11:1–18; 13:1–3; 14:23,27; 15:1–30; 16:4–5; 20:28; 1 Corinthians 5:1–5; 7:17; 16:1–3; 1 Timothy 4:14; 1 Peter 5:1–4

FOCAL TEXTS

Matthew 18:15–20; Acts 6:1–6; 13:1–3; 15:22; 1 Corinthians 5:1–5; 16:1–3

MAIN IDEA

"Baptists are democratic in their church government. Each local church is self-governing and independent in the management of its affairs."[1]

STUDY AIM

To explain how New Testament churches were organized and made decisions and what this teaches about church government today

QUICK READ

Baptists believe congregational church government best reflects New Testament practices, is demanded by biblical doctrines, and should be implemented in churches today. Baptists determine to resist all threats to its use and effectiveness.

I had completed a book on Baptist history in the Indonesian language. The book was ready for printing. The Indonesian seminary student who was drawing the picture for the book's cover was completing the picture. Everything was almost ready, but we still had not decided the book's exact title.

The student—in desperation, I think—indicated he could not finish the cover without a title. Again in desperation, he suggested, "What about calling it *The History of the Baptist Church*?"

Desperation, I suspect, drove me to respond, "Yes, let's just use that title!"

Another seminary student, who had heard the conversation, observed, "If what you taught us in the Baptist history class is correct, that would need to be *The Development of the Baptist Churches*, would it not?"

Of course the listening student was right. There is no "The Baptist Church." There are Baptist churches that often voluntarily join for cooperative efforts. Baptist historian Walter Shurden correctly notes that there is no "The Southern Baptist Church." One can properly speak of "The Methodist Church" or "The Presbyterian Church" but not of "The Baptist Church!"[2]

The Holy Spirit guided the early Christians to express their faith in Christ by banding together into spiritual fellowships that exhibited a church consciousness and corporate spiritual life (see Acts 2:1–4; 4:31; 8:14–17; 10:44). This corporate sense was rooted in the Jewish life in the synagogue. It came to fruit through their observance of the Greek concept of *ekklesia*, a word that refers to a community meeting for decision. Accepting this concept of the spiritual, corporate fellowship, Baptists have embraced congregational church government. Congregational church government both demands and allows democracy. Baptists believe New Testament churches were democratic bodies; they believe that churches today should be also.

Matthew 18:15–20 (NIV)

¹⁵"If your brother sins against you, go and show him his fault, just between the two of you. If he listens to you, you have won your brother over. ¹⁶But if he will not listen, take one or two others along, so that 'every matter may be established by the testimony of two or three witnesses.' ¹⁷If he refuses to listen to them, tell it to the church; and if he refuses to listen even to the church, treat him as you would a pagan or a tax collector.

¹⁸"I tell you the truth, whatever you bind on earth will be bound in heaven, and whatever you loose on earth will be loosed in heaven.

¹⁹"Again, I tell you that if two of you on earth agree about anything you ask for, it will be done for you by my Father in heaven. ²⁰For where two or three come together in my name, there am I with them."

Acts 6:1–6

¹In those days when the number of disciples was increasing, the Grecian Jews among them complained against the Hebraic Jews because their widows were being overlooked in the daily distribution of food. ²So the Twelve gathered all the disciples together and said, "It would not be right for us to neglect the ministry of the word of God in order to wait on tables. ³Brothers, choose seven men from among you who are known to be full of the Spirit and wisdom. We will turn this responsibility over to them ⁴and will give our attention to prayer and the ministry of the word."

⁵This proposal pleased the whole group. They chose Stephen, a man full of faith and of the Holy Spirit; also Philip, Procorus, Nicanor, Timon, Parmenas, and Nicolas from Antioch, a convert to Judaism. ⁶They presented these men to the apostles, who prayed and laid their hands on them.

Acts 13:1–3

¹In the church at Antioch there were prophets and teachers: Barnabas, Simeon called Niger, Lucius of Cyrene, Manaen (who had been brought up with Herod the tetrarch) and Saul. ²While they were worshiping the Lord and fasting, the Holy Spirit said, "Set apart for me Barnabas and Saul for the work to which I have called them." ³So after they had fasted and prayed, they placed their hands on them and sent them off.

Acts 15:22

Then the apostles and elders, with the whole church, decided to choose some of their own men and send them to Antioch with Paul and Barnabas. They chose Judas (called Barsabbas) and Silas, two men who were leaders among the brothers.

1 Corinthians 5:1–5

¹It is actually reported that there is sexual immorality among you, and of a kind that does not occur even among pagans: A man has his father's wife. ²And you are proud! Shouldn't you rather have been filled with grief and have put out of your fellowship the man who did this? ³Even though I am not physically present, I am with you in spirit. And I have already passed judgment on the one who did this, just as if I were present. ⁴When you are assembled in the name of our Lord Jesus and I am with you in spirit, and the power of our Lord Jesus is present, ⁵hand this man over to Satan, so that the sinful nature may be destroyed and his spirit saved on the day of the Lord.

1 Corinthians 16:1–3

¹Now about the collection for God's people: Do what I told the Galatian churches to do. ²On the first day of every week, each one of you should set aside a sum of money in keeping with his income, saving it up, so that when I come no collections will have to be made. ³Then, when I arrive, I will give letters of introduction to the men you approve and send them with your gift to Jerusalem.

The Nature of Congregational Church Government

The New Testament does not spell out precisely the details of church government. We can cite texts from various parts of the Bible that seem to support each of the major options for church government. Among these options, Baptists follow the congregational pattern, which they feel best reflects apostolic church polity and remains most faithful to biblical teachings.

In congregational church government, church authority centers in local, sovereign, independent congregations. Local churches committed to the congregational church government pattern have both the right and the responsibility to care for their own affairs under the guidance of Jesus Christ. No bishop, no convention, no pastor, no influential group (either local or national), no civil authority, and no association should dictate either the doctrines or the practices of a local church. No organization or group in Baptist life is superior to or legislates for the local congregations. Baptist churches place authority in the membership of the local fellowship under the guidance of Christ and allow no outside force to dictate either belief or practice.

The following teachings provide biblical foundation for Baptists' conviction that congregational church government represents the New Testament pattern and the best polity for local churches:

1. The New Testament churches were voluntary organisms. These fellowships were composed of members who, because of their own spiritual experience and decision, voluntarily joined with one another for the purpose of carrying out the will of God and the mission of Jesus under the guidance of the Holy Spirit (Acts 2:41–42,47).

New Testament churches of necessity must be composed of born-again, baptized believers. Only believers should be members of a Baptist church. The voluntary and regenerate nature of Christians demands a participative pattern in church relationships. Congregational church government alone, of the various options available, provides this opportunity for participation.

2. The New Testament churches were self-governing, spiritual democracies.
The word *democracy* comes from two Greek words that mean "rule of the
people." Jesus encouraged his followers not to insist on the term "rabbi"
for themselves but to recognize only Christ as their Master (teacher) and
all believers as brothers (Matthew 23:8). Thus, in the churches of the
New Testament, apostles could suggest solutions to problems, but all
important matters were referred to the congregations for settlement
(Acts 6:1–6; 1 Cor. 5:1–5; 2 Cor. 8:1–13).

This procedure clearly appeared in the appointment of workers to tend
to the relief help for the "widows" (Acts 6:1–6). A problem arose over the
neglect of the widows from the Greek-speaking group. This Greek-
speaking group was possibly Jews of the dispersion from the Greco-
Roman world, as over against the Hebraic Jews, who were probably
natives of Palestine and spoke Aramaic rather than Greek.[3] The apostles
suggested the number of men to serve in this role and their qualifications,
but the actual choice was left to the congregation.

Interestingly, the names of all seven chosen are Greek. This fact suggests that they all, with the exception of Nicolaus, who was likely a Gentile proselyte, stemmed from the Greek-speaking contingent in the
church. The congregational decision was attended by increased multipli-
cation of disciples including a large number of Jewish priests (6:7).

The democratic ideal in the New Testament churches clearly surfaces
in the accounts of the church at Antioch of Syria (13:1–3; 15:22). The
Holy Spirit spoke to the church in Antioch, instructing that Barnabas
and Saul be set apart for the missionary task. The entire church, not just
leaders, took part in the commissioning (13:3). Later, after the council
meeting in Jerusalem (15:1–21) had decided that Gentiles should not be
required to follow Jewish customary regulations in order to become
Christians, the apostles and elders "with the whole church" chose Judas
(called Barsabbas) and Silas to accompany Paul and Barnabas to relate the
council's advice to Antioch (15:22).

The teaching that the New Testament churches were self-governing,
spiritual democracies also finds support in the fact that the apostles

The Congregational Pattern of Church Government

- centers authority in church matters in the sovereign, independent body that has no direct, organic ties with any other church or governing body
- allows no hierarchical power to dictate either faith or practice to the local churches
- mirrors what seems to be the New Testament model
- allows cooperation with other bodies so long as there are no entangling alliances
- insists on the total freedom and responsibility of every member
- follows democratic processes in its deliberations

advised and exhorted the churches but the congregations determined their own courses of action.[4] The sense of 1 Corinthians 16:1–3 is that Paul encouraged, but did not order, the Christians in Corinth to participate in the offering to the famine-stricken believers in Jerusalem. The same encouragement without coercion for giving appears in Paul's injunctions to the Corinthians in 2 Corinthians 8:1–13. Note especially verse 8. We can see a similar pattern in Paul's urging forgiveness to an erring but repentant brother (2 Cor. 2:5–8).

3. *The New Testament churches cared for their own memberships and members.* Church membership and church discipline rested in the hands of the local congregations. Evidently the New Testament churches had the authority to receive or reject people from their memberships.[5] Paul advised the church in Rome to accept without passing judgment on the weak person, that is, one unsure of certain disputable doctrines (Rom. 14:1–2). He suggested to the church in Corinth that the one who had caused distress (grief) by his behavior had already been sufficiently punished *by the church as a whole* (2 Cor. 2:5–8). The New English Bible translates 2 Corinthians 2:6 as follows: "The penalty

on which the general meeting has agreed has met the offence well enough." Paul advised reinstating the erring member (2:7–8), but the actual discipline was the act of the entire church.

The accounts of church discipline in Matthew 18:15–20 and 1 Corinthians 5:1–5 further reveal the New Testament approach to church discipline. Jesus spoke of a believer who feels that another has wronged him or her (Matt. 18:15–20). The wronged believer should first go personally to the offender and try to work things out. Should this effort fail, the offended should take two or three others to hear the complaint. Should peace still be denied, the church should be asked to intercede. If the offender would not listen to the church, then the offender would be considered and treated as a "pagan or a tax-collector" (18:17). The passage underlines the importance of church decision-making.

Paul expressed a similar view in 1 Corinthians 5:1–5. There Paul spoke of the sinful behavior of a member of the church in Corinth. Paul rejected the immoral behavior, but he said to the membership that they, not he, should have "put out of your fellowship the man who did this" (1 Cor. 5:2). Again, the final responsibility and authority resided in the congregation.

When we consider these various New Testament passages, we see the background for Baptists' belief in congregational church government. Nothing less than congregational church government reflects the pattern of church authority residing in the entire membership and not in some outside power or force.

4. The New Testament churches were fellowships of mutual care and responsibility. Mutual care, worship, witness, and support represent the essence of the nature of New Testament churches. The Jerusalem fellowship continued in worship, fellowship, mutual sharing, and evangelism (Acts 2:42–47). These Christians continued to share, to worship, and, in the face of great threats, to witness boldly about Jesus (4:13–31).

Peter's experience with Cornelius (10:1–48) led to criticism by some Jewish Christians. Peter reported to the entire group. Upon hearing what God had done, they laid aside their complaints and declared that "God has granted even the Gentiles repentance unto life" (11:18).

Clearly, the believers and the churches in the New Testament demonstrated both the freedom and responsibility to determine, under Christ and in compliance with Scripture, their own membership, beliefs, and practices. Baptists are convinced that the congregational pattern of church government remains most faithful to and reflective of the New Testament plan.

These teachings compel Baptists to affirm congregational church government. They maintain that the same form of church government revealed in the New Testament remains the best for churches today.

Other options for church government exist and are employed today. Baptists respect those who follow other practices and work with them wherever possible. They do not agree with their patterns of church government, however. Baptists are convinced that the congregational plan best represents the New Testament pattern, best interfaces with basic biblical doctrines, and most adequately allows for the Lord's work.

The Foundations of Baptist Belief in Congregational Church Government

Although support for other forms of church government can be found in biblical passages, Baptists see the bulk of Scriptural evidence upholding congregational government. Even more important to the Baptist view are Scriptural doctrines that serve as foundations for congregational government.

1. The Priesthood of Every Believer. This New Testament doctrine means that every believer is a priest! Speaking of all Christians, Peter declared that God's people are "a chosen people, a royal priesthood, a holy nation, a people belonging to God" (1 Peter 2:9). Every believer has the possibility of coming face-to-face with God, boldly, with no mediator other than Christ (1 Timothy 2:5; Hebrews 4:16). He or she can pray directly to God in Jesus' name (John 14:13–14), can confess his or her sins directly to God (1 John 1:9), and can read and interpret the Scriptures as guided by the Holy Spirit (John 16:12–15). This priesthood of the believer involves both privilege and responsibility.

The priesthood of the believer means that all members serve as equals under God in the fellowship of a local church. Each believer, therefore, is obligated to serve as a priest on behalf of others. The doctrine of the priesthood of the believer constitutes a central affirmation of Baptists that must never be lost or its significance lowered.

In regard to congregational church government, this teaching means that every believer can seek and find God's will directly and therefore must be free to express his or her findings to the entire body. To ascertain God's directions, the church does well to hear the conclusions of every member and allow the full participation of the entire body of Christ. For these reasons, Baptists believe that authority in the church should be vested in the entire membership. W. R. White wrote, "The concept of the priesthood of every believer instead of a priestly class or caste makes democracy inevitable for the Lord's disciples."[6]

2. The Lordship of Jesus Christ. Consistently, the New Testament upholds the Lordship of Jesus Christ in all matters of Christian life and practice, both for individual believers and the churches. Since Christ is head and Lord of the Church, the churches seek to ascertain the mind of

Options for Church Government

- *The hierarchical (autocratic) pattern* exalts a human leader to a dominant position and gives this leader almost total authority or power.
- *The episcopal pattern* centers authority in the bishop or bishops.
- *The connectional pattern* centers authority in the combined voice of all the local congregations that subscribe to a common and prescribed creed.
- *The congregational pattern* centers authority in church matters in the sovereign, independent body that has no organic ties with any other church or governing body.

Christ in all matters of faith and practice (Ephesians 5:22–23). Freedom to respond to the Lordship of Christ in all circumstances is fundamental to the Christian faith, to human dignity, and to the proper functioning of Christ's churches. For this reason, the 1963 statement of "The Baptist Faith and Message" declares that "This church is an autonomous body, operating through democratic processes under the Lordship of Christ."[7]

Baptist understanding of the Lordship of Christ guides them directly to their stand on congregational church government. Every member has equal access to the Lord who is the head of the church (Colossians 1:18). No one person, no one group, no one power should take the place of Christ in the church.

3. The Autonomy of the Local Church. In order to remain an autonomous church, every congregation must be free from denominational, governmental, or other authoritarian pressures. Let us be clear about the meaning of church autonomy, however. As Charles Wade declares, "A church is not free to be or to do whatever it wants. It is called to be like Christ and do what Jesus would do."[8]

Local church autonomy means the church acts under compulsion and direction of Jesus Christ through the Holy Spirit rather than from outside pressure. Paul called on the church at Corinth to act in the "power of our Lord Jesus" (1 Cor. 5:4).

4. The Church As the Body of Christ. One picture or metaphor of the church is that of the body of Christ (Eph. 1:22–23; Rom. 12:4–5; 1 Cor. 12:12–31). Charles Wade calls this image the most dominant picture of the church in the New Testament.[9] The central theme in this metaphor is that of the many parts working together in unity and power to accomplish the overall purpose of the body. The concept of the church as the body of Christ points toward the understanding of the church as an organism, with every part important and necessary.

Since the church is a body, a living organism, every part must function for the whole to be strong and accomplish its task. Congregational church government provides a more certain avenue for such mutual action and functioning. The biblical teaching of the church as the body of Christ gives support to the idea of democratic church government.

These biblical teachings—the priesthood of believers, the Lordship of Christ, the autonomy of the local church, and the church as the body of Christ—have motivated Baptists to accept, insist on, promote, and maintain the congregational mode of church government as the most theologically sound and appropriate approach to church polity.

Threats to Congregational Church Government

Although Baptists traditionally hold strongly to the concept of congregational church government, threats to its continued practice and effectiveness exist—both from outside and inside the Baptist family. Consider the following threats.

1. Passivity Among Christians and Churches. Baptist historian Walter Shurden notes passivity as perhaps the most perennial and serious threat to the congregational church government pattern.[10] Freedom and autonomy involve both liberty and responsibility. To simply "go along" with what other churches or leaders are saying or doing without comparing these actions and teachings with the genuine source of authority, the Bible, can often lead to accepting unbiblical teachings and practices or to abstaining from biblically mandated actions and teachings. When Christians and churches become passive and refuse to take necessary and at times unpopular stands, congregational church government can be lost or find its effectiveness diminished.

2. Authoritarianism Among Leaders and Churches. Another threat to congregational church government and its effectiveness stems from an overly aggressive authoritarianism by church leaders—either clergy or laity. Pastoral authority that assumes a demanding, controlling, ruling function seriously threatens New Testament church life. The New Testament does advise Christians to remember and respect their spiritual leaders (Hebrews 13:7). Clergy leaders, however, must remember that church leaders are to be servants rather than overlords (Matt. 20:25–26). Church leaders are to serve willingly, without desire for financial gain, and as overseers rather than overlords (1 Pet. 5:1–4).

By the same token, lay leaders in the churches can often seize power and authority so as to concentrate church decision-making in the hands of a few. This approach equally threatens congregational church government. The church, not a minority in the church, best expresses the will of Christ.

Authoritarianism prevents congregational church government from functioning. No denomination or local congregation can become what God wills it to be and do apart from the full expression of church freedom. Church members must guard congregational church government as a sacred trust. Any hierarchy destroys congregationalism and the historic Baptist concept of the equality of believers in the local church.[11]

These and other threats to the practice of congregational church government alert Baptists to the danger of such encroachment on the pattern. Awareness of such threats should strengthen our resolve to maintain the biblical plan and resist any erosion of congregational church government.

Applying the Teaching

Although various options for church government exist, Baptists remain convinced that congregational church government best reflects the New Testament pattern and constitutes the best plan for churches today. The teaching of congregational church government clearly springs both from direct biblical accounts of New Testament churches and from the implications of doctrines concerning the church.

Threats to congregational church government exist in the passivity of Christians and churches and in authoritarianism on the part of either clergy or lay church members. Baptists must be willing to stand against any encroachment, from within or without the church, on the practice of congregational church government. The New Testament churches were congregational; churches today do well to follow their example.

QUESTIONS

1. What theological teachings indicate that authoritarian rule by either pastor, a group of lay persons, or a denominational entity would violate biblical teachings relating to congregational church government?

2. Which threat to congregational church government do you consider most serious? Would you add other threats?

3. Of the reasons for using congregational church government, which do you consider most valid? Which, if any, would you see as less valid?

4. To what extent does your church follows the principles of congregational church government? What evidence do you see for your answer? What could be done to improve the situation if it needs improving?

Notes

1. Walter Thomas Conner, *Christian Doctrine* (Nashville, Tennessee: Broadman Press, 1937), 266.
2. Walter B. Shurden, *The Baptist Identity: Four Fragile Freedoms* (Macon, GA: Smyth & Helwys, 1993), 38–39.
3. Curtis Vaughan, *Acts: A Study Guide Commentary* (Grand Rapids: Zondervan, 1974), 44.
4. Herschel H. Hobbs, *What Baptists Believe* (Nashville: Convention Press, 1964), 79.
5. W. R. White, *Baptist Distinctives* (Nashville: Convention Press, 1946), 38.
6. White, *Baptist Distinctives*, 38.
7. Article 6, "The Baptist Faith and Message," 1963.
8. Charles R. Wade, with Lee and Carol Bowman, *The Jesus Principle: Building Churches in the Likeness of Christ* (Arlington, TX: Clear Stream Publishing Inc., 1998), 79.
9. Wade, *The Jesus Principle*, 74.
10. Shurden, *The Baptist Identity*, 38.
11. Shurden, *The Baptist Identity*, 38.

The Deity and Lordship of Jesus Christ

BACKGROUND SCRIPTURES

Psalm 2:7; 110:1; Isaiah 7:14; 53; Matthew 1:18–23; 3:17; 8:29; 11:25–30; 14:33; 16:13–16, 27; 17:1–8; 27:1—28:6, 19; Mark 1:1; 3:11; Luke 1:35; 4:41; 22:70; 24:46; John 1:1–18, 29; 5:31–47; 10:30–39; 11:25–27; 12:44–50; 14:7–11; 16:15–16, 28; 17:1–5, 21–22; 20:1–20, 28; Acts 1:9; 2:22–24; 7:55–56; 9:4–5, 20; Romans 1:1–6; 3:23–26; 5:6–21; 8:1–3, 34; 10:4; 1 Corinthians 1:30; 2:2; 8:6; 15:1–8, 24–28; 2 Corinthians 5:19–21; Galatians 4:4–5; Ephesians 1:18–23; 3:11; 4:7–10; Philippians 2:5–11; Colossians 1:13–22; 2:9; 1 Thessalonians 4:14–18; 1 Timothy 2:5–6; Titus 2:13–14; Hebrews 1:1–3; 4:14–15; 7:14–28; 9:12–15, 24–28; 12:2; 13:8; 1 Peter 2:21–25; 3:21–22; 1 John 1:7–9; 3:2; 4:14–15; 5:9; 2 John 7–9; Revelation 1:13–16; 5:1–14; 12:10–11; 13:8; 19:16

FOCAL TEXTS

Matthew 16:13–16; John 1:1–5, 14; 10:30–38; 20:28; Philippians 2:5–11; Colossians 2:9; Revelation 5:1–14

MAIN IDEA

"The Christ of the New Testament is not a man deified by his zealous disciples, but the eternal Son of God who voluntarily became man to redeem lost humanity."[1]

STUDY AIM

To state what the New Testament teaches about Jesus' deity and lordship

QUICK READ

Jesus Christ is God in human flesh. He is both fully God and fully human. As God, he is co-equal and co-eternal with God the Father and God the Holy Spirit.

An *iota* is the smallest letter in the Greek alphabet, but there was a time when the whole Roman Empire was divided over the question of just "one iota." About the time that Christianity was declared the official religion of the Roman Empire, the emperor Constantine called for a council of bishops to convene in the city of Nicea in the summer of 325 A.D. The purpose of the meeting was to settle a dispute that threatened the unity of the church and the empire.

A young priest from Egypt named Arius had begun to teach that Christ had been created by God and thus was not fully divine. For this heresy the Egyptian bishops "unfrocked" Arius. Some leaders of the church disagreed with the action. The dispute grew.

In an attempt to settle the question, Constantine convened the first great church council. The orthodox believers insisted that Christ is fully divine and of the same essence as God the Father. The term in the Greek language is *homo-ousian*—that is, the "same essence." Those following Arius contended that Christ was of a different essence from God, using the term *hetero-ousian*.

As many as 318 bishops attended the council, and some 300 of them agreed that Christ is of the same essence (*homo-ousian*). However, 17 of them refused to sign the document unless one subtle compromise was made. The letter *iota* had to be added to the defining word. The word would then become *homoi-ousian*. That word means "similar essence" instead of the "same essence." The decision of the council hinged on the one Greek letter, *iota*.

The majority refused to insert that little Greek letter and thus agree that Christ was less than fully God. Thus the council declared Arianism to be heresy. The Council at Nicea issued the following statement:

> We believe in one God, the Father All-mighty, maker of all things visible or invisible; and in one Lord Jesus Christ, the Son of God, begotten . . . not made, being of one essence [*homo-ousian*] with the Father . . . who for us . . . and our salvation came down and was made

flesh, was made man, suffered, rose again the third day, ascended into heaven, and comes to judge the quick and the dead . . . .[2]

Church historian Philip Schaff said of Nicea, "It is the first and most venerable of the ecumenical synods, and next to the apostolic council at Jerusalem the most important and the most illustrious of all the councils of Christendom."[3]

Many other controversies about the nature and work of Christ have arisen across the centuries of Christian history. Even today the answer to the question that still distinguishes true Christianity is, "Who is Christ?"

We Baptists do not derive our doctrines from creeds or councils but from the Bible, which is the Word of God, truth without mixture of error. There is no more foundational doctrine for Baptists than the deity and lordship of Christ our Savior. In this study we will look at just a few of the many Scriptures that deal with the person and work of Christ.

Who Is Jesus? (Matthew 16:13–16)

In preparing his disciples for his impending crucifixion, Jesus asked what the latest public opinion polls said about him. While the religious leaders regarded Jesus as a blasphemer against God (Matthew 9:3), average people were complimentary of Jesus.

Some thought Jesus to be John the Baptist who had risen from the dead as Herod feared (14:2). Others believed Jesus to be Elijah. It was prophesied in Malachi 4:5 that Elijah would precede and prepare the way for the Messiah. Another suggestion was that Jesus was Jeremiah who had returned.

In the next verse the Master pointedly changed the question. He asked, "But who do you say that I am?" (16:15). Peter declared that Jesus was the long awaited Anointed One, the Christ who is the Son of the Living God. By this confession, Peter revealed that he understood that Jesus is God.

Matthew 16:13–16 (NASB)

[13]Now when Jesus came into the district of Caesarea Philippi, He was asking His disciples, "Who do people say that the Son of Man is?" [14]And they said, "Some say John the Baptist; and others, Elijah; but still others, Jeremiah, or one of the prophets." [15]He said to them, "But who do you say that I am?" [16]Simon Peter answered, "You are the Christ, the Son of the living God."

John 1:1–5, 14

[1]In the beginning was the Word, and the Word was with God, and the Word was God. [2]He was in the beginning with God. [3]All things came into being through Him, and apart from Him nothing came into being that has come into being. [4]In Him was life, and the life was the Light of men. [5]The Light shines in the darkness, and the darkness did not comprehend it.

• •

[14]And the Word became flesh, and dwelt among us, and we saw His glory, glory as of the only begotten from the Father, full of grace and truth.

John 10:30–38

[30]"I and the Father are one."
[31]The Jews picked up stones again to stone Him. [32]Jesus answered them, "I showed you many good works from the Father; for which of them are you stoning Me?" [33]The Jews answered Him, "For a good work we do not stone You, but for blasphemy; and because You, being a man, make Yourself out to be God." [34]Jesus answered them, "Has it not been written in your Law, 'I SAID, YOU ARE GODS'? [35]"If he called them gods, to whom the word of God came (and the Scripture cannot be broken), [36]do you say of Him, whom the Father sanctified and sent into the world, 'You are blaspheming,' because I said, 'I am the Son of God'? [37]"If I do

not do the works of My Father, do not believe Me; [38]but if I do them, though you do not believe Me, believe the works, so that you may know and understand that the Father is in Me, and I in the Father."

John 20:28

Thomas answered and said to Him, "My Lord and my God!"

Philippians 2:5–11

[5]Have this attitude in yourselves which was also in Christ Jesus, [6]who, although He existed in the form of God, did not regard equality with God a thing to be grasped, [7]but emptied Himself, taking the form of a bond-servant, and being made in the likeness of men. [8]Being found in appearance as a man, He humbled Himself by becoming obedient to the point of death, even death on a cross. [9]For this reason also, God highly exalted Him, and bestowed on Him the name which is above every name, [10]so that at the name of Jesus EVERY KNEE WILL BOW, of those who are in heaven and on earth and under the earth, [11]and that every tongue will confess that Jesus Christ is Lord, to the glory of God the Father.

Colossians 2:9

For in Him all the fullness of Deity dwells in bodily form . . . .

Revelation 5:1–14

[1]I saw in the right hand of Him who sat on the throne a book written inside and on the back, sealed up with seven seals. [2]And I saw a strong angel proclaiming with a loud voice, "Who is worthy to open the book and to break its seals?" [3]And no one in heaven or on the earth or under the earth was able to open the book or to look into it. [4]Then I began to weep greatly because no one was found worthy to open the book or to look into it; [5]and one of the elders said to me, "Stop weeping; behold, the

Lion that is from the tribe of Judah, the Root of David, has overcome so as to open the book and its seven seals."

⁶And I saw between the throne (with the four living creatures) and the elders a Lamb standing, as if slain, having seven horns and seven eyes, which are the seven Spirits of God, sent out into all the earth. ⁷And He came and took the book out of the right hand of Him who sat on the throne. ⁸When He had taken the book, the four living creatures and the twenty-four elders fell down before the Lamb, each one holding a harp and golden bowls full of incense, which are the prayers of the saints. ⁹And they sang a new song, saying,

> "Worthy are You to take the book and to break its seals; for You were slain, and purchased for God with Your blood men from every tribe and tongue and people and nation.
>
> ¹⁰ "You have made them to be a kingdom and priests to our God; and they will reign upon the earth."

¹¹Then I looked, and I heard the voice of many angels around the throne and the living creatures and the elders; and the number of them was myriads of myriads, and thousands of thousands, ¹²saying with a loud voice,

> "Worthy is the Lamb that was slain to receive power and riches and wisdom and might and honor and glory and blessing."

¹³And every created thing which is in heaven and on the earth and under the earth and on the sea, and all things in them, I heard saying,

> "To Him who sits on the throne, and to the Lamb, be blessing and honor and glory and dominion forever and ever."

¹⁴And the four living creatures kept saying, "Amen." And the elders fell down and worshiped.

Who Is Christ? (John 1:1–5, 14)

The first chapter of John begins with these words, "In the beginning was the Word, and the Word was with God, and the Word was God" (John 1:1). The Lord Jesus Christ is the "Word" in John 1:1. He is the first and last word from God. He is "the Alpha and the Omega" (Revelation 1:8).

While God has spoken through the prophets, he has been most personally revealed in the Lord Jesus Christ (Hebrews 1:1–3).

As we study John 1:1–5, 14, let us consider first what these verses teach us about the deity of Christ. John 1:1–5 contains seven descriptions of Christ (the Word). These descriptions reveal that he is God.

- "In the beginning . . . the Word was God" (John 1:1). Christ is *co-eternal* with God. At the time of creation, the Word was already with God. Before anything was created, Christ was already in existence. Therefore, he is not a created being. He preceded creation.

- This phrase also reveals the *distinct personality* of Jesus Christ. He "was with God" (1:1). There is one God, and there are three distinct persons in God: Father, Son, and Holy Spirit. It is impossible for the finite mind to comprehend the doctrine of the "trinity" that is taught so clearly in Scripture. Many explanations have been given, but none are completely adequate.

- Christ is *co-equal* with God. Christ did not become God; he already was God. Christ is not inferior to God the Father. Any teaching that claims that the Lord Jesus Christ is less than God is unbiblical and untrue. The Word was not "a" God. Neither was the Word "the" God, which would eliminate the other persons in the Godhead. Nor was he merely "of" God, but in the beginning he was already in his nature and essence fully and completely God.

- Christ is *changeless.* "He was in the beginning with God" (John 1:2). "Jesus Christ the same yesterday, and to day, and for ever" (Hebrews 13:8, KJV).

- Christ is *creator.* "All things were made by him; and without him was not anything made that was made" (John 1:3, KJV; see also Colossians 1:15–17).

- Christ is the *life-source.* "In him was life" (John 1:4). First, Christ created the material universe, and then he brought living organisms into being.

One of the legends making the rounds on the Internet describes a meeting of God and a scientist who had recently been successful in cloning an animal. In the story, the scientist challenged God, saying, "I can create human life." According to the story, God replied, "Go ahead and try." With that the scientist reached down and scooped up a handful of dirt. God supposedly replied, "Wait a minute. Get your own dirt."

Not only is Christ the origin of all life, but he is the creator and sole proprietor of the new life that is eternal life. "I am . . . the life" (14:6).

- Christ is the *source of light* (see 1:4b–5). "God is Light, and in Him there is no darkness at all" (1 John 1:5). Jesus clearly said, "'I am the Light of the world; he who follows Me will not walk in the darkness, but will have the Light of life'" (John 8:12).

Consider now what John 1:14 teaches us about the humanity of Christ. Not only was Christ fully God, but he also became fully human and "dwelt" or "tabernacled" among us. The word translated "dwell" literally means "to tabernacle" or "to put up a tent."

Consider these five ways in which the Old Testament tabernacle symbolizes the first coming of Christ, when the Word became flesh.

(1) The tabernacle was intended to be temporary, as was the first coming of Christ.

(2) The tabernacle was to be used in the wilderness even as Christ endured the wilderness in his first coming.

The Lord Jesus Christ

The word "Lord" declares Jesus' divinity. The word "Jesus" designates his humanity. The word "Christ" describes his office as prophet, priest, and king. As prophet, he is the Word of God. As priest, he offered himself as the atoning sacrifice for sin. As king, he is sovereign over all creation.

(3) The tabernacle was very plain on the outside, but it was glorious on the inside, just as there was no outward beauty in Christ that we should desire him (Isaiah 53:2).

(4) The tabernacle was God's temporary dwelling place on earth even as the fullness of God dwelled in Christ bodily.

(5) The tabernacle was the place of sacrifice for sin even as Christ sacrificed himself in his own body on the cross (Hebrews 10:12).[4]

Christ Reveals His Deity (John 10:30-38)

Christ himself gave testimony to his deity. He said, "I and my father are one" (John 10:30, KJV). The religious leaders understood his meaning well, for they accused Jesus of claiming to be God.

Jesus did not often claim to be God because truth must be established in the mouth of two witnesses (Deuteronomy 19:15). In John 5:31–47 Jesus cited four independent witnesses who would testify that he is God.

(1) John the Baptist pointed to Jesus as the Lamb of God who would take away the sin of the world (John 5:33–35; see 1:29).

(2) The very works of Christ did bear witness that he is one with the Father (5:36).

(3) God the Father testified of Christ (5:37; see also Matthew 3:17).

(4) The Scriptures bear witness of Christ (John 5:39–47).

Thomas Declares the Deity of Christ (John 20:28)

On the evening of resurrection day, ten of the apostles met in the upper room. Two were absent. Judas Iscariot had hanged himself, and Thomas was not there.

When the disciples assembled a week later, Thomas was present with them. Again Christ appeared in their midst and invited Thomas,

The Use of "Word"

The average Jewish person of Jesus' day spoke the Aramaic language. The translations of Old Testament passages into Aramaic were called "targums." In order to preserve the glory of the Almighty, the term "Word of God" was used whenever God acted with humans or in a human way. Here are just two examples from the targums. In Genesis 3:8–9 instead of "they heard the voice of the Lord God," the targums say that they heard the voice of "the word of the Lord God." Instead of "God called unto Adam," the targums say that "the word of the Lord called unto Adam." This term "the word of the Lord" occurred as many as 150 times in a single targum of the Pentateuch.[6]

To the Greeks, "logos," which means "word," was also a well known term. Greek philosophers taught that the "logos" gave order and unity to the world. To the Greeks then, it is as if John were saying, I want to introduce your "logos" to you. He is the Christ.

"'Reach hither thy finger, and behold my hands; and reach hither thy hand, and thrust it into my side: and be not faithless, but believing'" (John 20:27, KJV).

There is no indication that Thomas touched the hands or the side of the Savior, but he openly confessed, "My Lord and my God!" (John 20:28). If Christ had not been God, he would have corrected Thomas. Christ accepted this justifiable praise.

Christ Is Equal with God (Philippians 2:5–11)

This passage in Philippians is one of the most glorious descriptions of the voluntary descent from heaven of the incarnate God in order to bear the sins of the world in his body on the cross. Of this passage F. B. Meyer says, "In the whole range of Scripture this paragraph stands in almost unapproachable and unexampled majesty. There is no passage where the extremes of our Savior's majesty and humility are brought into such abrupt connection."[5]

Christ was in his very nature all the fullness of God, but he did not consider that he should clutch and retain this exalted position. He was "equal with God" (Philippians 2:6, KJV). Even so he "emptied Himself," laid aside his garments of glory, and took the form of a servant (2:7). One would think that if the Son of God were to come to earth, he would come with all the trappings that would befit the office. He could have far superseded the triumphal entry of a Roman emperor. Instead he worked in a carpenter shop (Mark 6:3) and even washed the feet of his self-seeking disciples (John 13:5).

Jesus reached the depths of shameful treatment in the crucifixion, "even death on a cross" (Phil. 2:8). *The deepest humiliation ever endured produced the greatest work ever accomplished, making redemption available to the human race.* Therefore God has highly exalted the one who voluntarily humbled himself. God has caused the name "Jesus" to be exalted above every other name. One day every knee shall bow and every tongue shall confess that Jesus Christ is Lord. In this, God the Father will be glorified (see 2:9–10).

Christ Is the Fullness of God (Colossians 2:9)

The Book of Colossians was written to warn Christians about false logic and philosophy that produced theological and practical errors. False teachers taught that matter is the origin and vehicle of evil. This false doctrine produced the theological error that Christ could not have appeared in the flesh since flesh is evil. Many levels of intermediary beings between God and human beings were required and worshiped in this system. The practical error was that a rigid ascetic discipline was required to overcome the evil properties of the physical and material.

Both errors could be overcome with the understanding that in Christ dwells all the fullness of God in bodily form (Colossians 2:9). He is creator of all things in heaven and earth, "visible and invisible" (1:16). He is redeemer through "the blood of His cross" (1:20). All the fullness of God dwells in Christ (1:19).

A good test for any religion is how it regards Christ. Any religion that makes Christ in any way inferior to God the Father or requires the observance of rules and rituals for salvation is false.

True or False Religions?

If members of another religion were to come to your door and attempt to convince you to accept their doctrine, could you give a reason for your faith? Could you tell truth from error? How can you tell whether a religion claiming to be Christian is true or false? Here are two of the tests that can be applied.

1. What is its source of religious authority? Is it the Bible only, or does that religion have other revelations, sacred books, and other writings as sources of doctrine equal or superior to the Bible? If there is any authority other than the Bible as the source of its doctrine, then this religion is not the true Christian faith.

2. What is the Christology of the religious denomination? What do they believe about the nature of Christ? If they believe that Christ is less than co-equal and co-eternal with God, or that Christ is not God incarnate in the flesh, then this is false Christianity.

This understanding is tremendously important because someday your children, your brother or sister, or your associate may become confused by the false claims of other religious groups. If a religion fails these tests at any point, then beware (see 1 John 2:22–23).

Christ Is Glorified in Heaven (Revelation 5:1–14)

In Revelation 5:1–14, there is a majestic picture of heaven. Not only is Christ, the Lamb of God, receiving praise from every creature, but he also is receiving praise co-equal with God upon the throne.

Your Lord and Your God?

The enemies of Christ said he was demented and demonic. The secular world may think of him as a great leader and religious martyr. Many religious people give intellectual assent that he is the Christ, the Son of the living God. Even that answer is inadequate without commitment to him as Lord. The saving answer is that of Thomas. Jesus is "*My* Lord and *My* God" (John 20:28). Have you confessed Jesus as your Lord and your God?

QUESTIONS

1. Why did Jesus not often claim to be God?

2. What is the difference between the confessions of Simon Peter and Thomas?

3. What experiences or circumstances led you to confess Christ as your Lord and your God?

Notes

1. Walter Thomas Conner, *Christian Doctrine* (Nashville, Tennessee: Broadman Press, 1937), 64.
2. Cited in W. Durant, *Caesar and Christ* (New York: Simon and Schuster, 1944), 665.
3. P. Schaff, *History of the Christian Church*, vol. II (Grand Rapids, Michigan: W. B. Eerdmans, 1910), 630.
4. Adapted from A. W. Pink, *Exposition of the Gospel of John* (Grand Rapids, Michigan: Zondervan Publishing House, 1945), 34–37.
5. F.B. Meyer, *The Epistle to the Philippians* (Grand Rapids, Michigan: Baker Book House, 1952), 81.
6. A. Plummer, *The Gospel According to St. John* (Cambridge: The University Press, 1899), 61.

Evangelism and Missions: The Great Commission

BACKGROUND SCRIPTURES

Genesis 12:1–3; Exodus 19:3–6; Isaiah 6:1–8; Matthew 9:37–38; 10:5–15; 13:8–30,37–43; 16:19; 22:9–10; 24:14; 28:18–20; Luke 10:1–18; 24:46–53; John 14:11–12; 15:7–8,16; 17:15; 20:21; Acts 1:8; 2; 8:26–40; 10:42–48; 13:2–3; Romans 10:1–15; Ephesians 3:1–11; 1 Thessalonians 1:8; 2 Timothy 4:5; Hebrews 2:1–3; 11:39—12:2; 1 Peter 2:4–10; Revelation 22:17

FOCAL TEXTS

Genesis 12:1–3; Exodus 19:5–6; Matthew 28:18–20; John 20:21; Acts 1:8; Romans 10:13–15

MAIN IDEA

"Missions/evangelism finds its ultimate source in the heart of God."[1]

STUDY AIM

To tell why evangelism and missions are essential tasks of churches and individual Christians

QUICK READ

Missions/evangelism is an essential task of Christ's church because God desires all people to be saved; salvation meets the ultimate human need; and Christ's commission obviously includes missions. Evangelism happens only in the Spirit's power.

Some years ago, my family visited Yellowstone National Park and watched as "Old Faithful" gushed water high into the air. We were impressed. I noted two cartoons on a wall in the area. Both showed people standing and watching "Old Faithful." In one cartoon, a watcher said, "Is that all it does?" In the second cartoon, a speaker said, "But what's it good for?"

Have you ever looked at the church (or a church) and asked, "Is that all it does?" Or have you inquired, "What's it really good for?" This study seeks to answer both questions—what do churches do and what are they good for!

Jesus called his church to carry forward his redemptive plan for all the people of the world. The task of the church includes proclaiming by word and deed the gospel of Jesus Christ, guiding believers into continuing growth and development in Christ, ministering to the needs of people in the communities, influencing the world toward right living, and preparing God's people for the Second Coming of the Lord Jesus Christ.

A prominent part of this overall task of the church relates to evangelism and missions, the effort designed to lead people to faith and salvation. While the full meaning of evangelism and missions includes everything the church does, in this study we will center on the mission of the church to bring people to saving faith in Jesus. No real difference exists between missions and evangelism. The two terms relate to the same task of bringing lost people to faith in Christ.

The Bible indicates that evangelism/missions constitutes an essential task both of the church and of individual Christians. Baptists affirm this task in "The Baptist Faith and Message": "It is the duty and privilege of every follower of Christ and every church of the Lord Jesus Christ to endeavor to make disciples of all nations."[2] Consider some reasons that missions/evangelism rests at the heart of the task of the church of Jesus Christ.

Genesis 12:1–3 (NIV)

The LORD had said to Abram, "Leave your country, your people and your father's household and go to the land I will show you.
² "I will make you into a great nation
   and I will bless you;
 I will make your name great,
   and you will be a blessing.
³ I will bless those who bless you,
   and whoever curses you I will curse;
 and all peoples on earth
   will be blessed through you."

Exodus 19:5–6

⁵Now if you obey me fully and keep my covenant, then out of all nations you will be my treasured possession. Although the whole earth is mine, ⁶you will be for me a kingdom of priests and a holy nation.' These are the words you are to speak to the Israelites."

Matthew 28:18–20

¹⁸Then Jesus came to them and said, "All authority in heaven and on earth has been given to me. ¹⁹Therefore go and make disciples of all nations, baptizing them in the name of the Father and of the Son and of the Holy Spirit, ²⁰and teaching them to obey everything I have commanded you. And surely I am with you always, to the very end of the age."

John 20:21

Again Jesus said, "Peace be with you! As the Father has sent me, I am sending you."

Acts 1:8

"But you will receive power when the Holy Spirit comes on you; and you will be my witnesses in Jerusalem, and in all Judea and Samaria, and to the ends of the earth."

Romans 10:13–15

[13]for, "Everyone who calls on the name of the Lord will be saved."
[14]How, then, can they call on the one they have not believed in? And how can they believe in the one of whom they have not heard? And how can they hear without someone preaching to them? [15]And how can they preach unless they are sent? As it is written, "How beautiful are the feet of those who bring good news!"

Missions/Evangelism Begins with the Loving Desire of God (Genesis 12:1–3; Exodus 19:5–6)

We know that missions/evangelism constitute an essential task of churches and Christians because the stimulus for the effort begins in God's loving desire to bring people to saving faith. Far from being a merely human endeavor, missions/evangelism springs from God's awesome desire to save sinful humanity and from God's direct call that his people be involved in this missionary effort (see Genesis 12:1–3; Exodus 19:5–6; Isaiah 49:6; Mark 10:45; John 3:16; Acts 1:8).

God announced his desire for all humanity and his intention that his people share the divine message of love with all humankind in his call of Abram (Abraham) in Genesis 12:1–3. Note the expression, "The Lord had said" (Gen. 12:1). This expression may indicate a renewal of the call first given in Haran as seen in Genesis 11:31–32.

The call to Abram required a radical separation from family, land, and natural roots in obedience to God. The word "make" indicates that God was forming a covenant with Abram (12:2). If Abram remained obedient, this covenant promised a great nation (many, innumerable descendants), a blessing (God would make Abram and his people happy, safe, successful, and prosperous), and a great name (the family would be known over the entire world). The selection of Abram and his family was not for Abram's benefit. Rather, the reason for the selection was that in Abram and his descendants "all peoples on earth will be blessed through you" (12:3).

God's call is always a call to share and bless, not to hold and be blessed. No person or group should consider the relationship with God only as a source of benefit. The blessings of God demand stewardship and responsibility. "We demonstrate the value of God's gifts more when we share them than when we possess them."[3] God's people must, therefore, be a missionary people. God calls and blesses his people *so that* they can realize God's mission to reach all peoples.

Few passages more stress the missionary/evangelistic message of the Bible than Exodus 19:3–6. There God declared that his people, Israel, were to be priests, that is, people who mediated between God and their fellow human beings to proclaim God's offer of salvation. The Lord reminded the people of how he had delivered them from Egypt. He had guided and protected them like an eagle guiding and protecting the fledgling that was learning to fly. God promised that if the people obeyed and followed him, he would make them his own "treasured possession . . . a kingdom of priests and a holy nation" among all the peoples of the earth (Exod. 19:3).

The entire nation of Israel was to become "priests" and serve as mediators between God and the nations—the other peoples of the world. This responsibility and opportunity now applies to the entire body of Christ's people. This great blessing given to God's people was—and is—never to be used exclusively for themselves. Christians today are God's people; they have experienced God's great and miraculous acts. They should, therefore, share God's love and salvation with all peoples and remain totally committed to him.

God has revealed his desire for all humankind throughout Scripture. In his message through Isaiah, God said, "'I will also make you a light for the Gentiles, that you may bring my salvation to the ends of the earth'" (Isaiah 49:6). Jesus enjoined his followers to pray that the Lord of the harvest would send out workers to the fields, fields that contain plentiful fruit (Matthew 9:37–38). The Lord sent out his followers to preach the message to the "lost sheep of Israel" (Matt. 10:5–15). He encouraged his followers by promising that the good soil would produce good fruit that would be harvested (13:1–43). The Master further indicated the Father's great desire for lost humanity in the three wonderful parables of love for the lost—the lost sheep, the lost coin, and the lost son (Luke 15:1–32). John reflected this same divine desire in John 3:16. Paul mirrored God's desire in declaring that his heart's desire for the Israelites was "that they may be saved" (Romans 10:1).

Evangelism/missions remains a central and essential task of the church because the ultimate source for the effort springs directly from the revealed nature of God himself. God wants his lost children found and brought back to his fold.

Evangelism/Missions Meets the Ultimate Human Need (Romans 10:13–15)

Evangelism/missions is an essential task of the church because in these ministries, Christians bring sinful humanity to the one solution to their ultimate need. Jesus sent his followers to the "lost sheep of the house of Israel" (Matt. 10:5–15). The Lord intends that the message of his salvation be preached to all peoples before the end (24:14). The apostle Paul showed this ultimate human need when he declared that all people have sinned and remain, in their unforgiven state, under the judgment of God (Rom. 3:21–31; 2 Cor. 5:11–21; Ephesians 2:1–10). Peter insisted that salvation was only in the name of Jesus (Acts 4:12). Sinful, unrepentant humans stand lost and condemned before God and have hope only in Christ.

Quotes on the Evangelistic/Missionary Task of the Church

"The church exists by mission just as fire exists by burning."
— EMIL BRUNNER, *THE WORD AND THE WORLD*, PAGE 108.

"The rankest heresy of which a church can be guilty is to ignore or repudiate its missionary obligation. It is impossible for one to accept the divine authority of the New Testament and deny the missionary function of the church, unless he is blinded by ignorance and prejudice."
— H. E. DANA, *A MANUAL OF ECCLESIOLOGY*, PAGE 233.

"The church that is not missionary in spirit and practice does not deserve the ground upon which its building stands."
— GEORGE W. TRUETT, CITED IN HERSCHEL HOBBS, *WHAT BAPTISTS BELIEVE*, PAGE 89.

Paul's heart's desire and prayer to God for his people, Israel, was "that they may be saved" (Rom. 10:1). The apostle's message in Romans 10:1–12 may be summed up in these three statements: (1) Although the Israelites were religious and sought strenuously to find a way to right-standing with God in human ritual, they remained lost because their quest was to no avail (10:1–2). (2) Their failure to reach right standing with God resulted from the fact that they attempted to establish this position through their own, human actions (10:2–7). (3) A new and living way had been provided through Christ. Anyone who repented of his or her sin, confessed Jesus as Lord, and believed in his or her heart the truth of the gospel would be saved (10:8–12).

The people of Israel, though religious, stood in need of God's salvation. Salvation in Christ alone could meet the ultimate human need— that is, the need to overcome the sin barrier and find rightstanding with God. The church must accept, as an essential task, that of proclaiming this message of salvation and guiding lost and unsaved people into this new relationship with God in Christ.

Paul next asked how people could call upon him of whom they had not heard. Paul then declared to Christians and churches that their responsibility included the task of proclaiming Christ, by word and by deed, to the lost (10:13–15). Herschel Hobbs wrote, " . . . the responsibility to tell the good news rested upon those who had heard it. It has been and always will be this way. Those who have received the gospel are to share it."[4]

An essential task of every Christian and every church is evangelism/ missions. The urgent need of salvation among the peoples of the earth

William Carey (1761–1834)— The "Heart and Soul"[9] of Baptists' Initial Emphasis on Missions

In 1792, at the Baptist association meeting held in Nottingham, England, a young cobbler and preacher named William Carey preached what has been called the "Deathless Sermon." At that time, the antimissionary spirit of hyper-Calvinist theology dominated the thought of Baptists. Carey's text was Isaiah 54:2–3, and the theme of his message was "Expect great things from God; attempt great things for God." Carey's sermon called attention to the imperative of missions.

The sermon greatly impressed Carey's hearers. As is so often the case, however, it appeared that nothing would be done about it. At the business session the next day, many cautioned against taking immediate action.

Andrew Fuller, a greatly respected preacher, was sitting beside Carey. Carey turned and pleaded with him, "Is there nothing again going to be done, sir?" Fuller rose and spoke for missions. Fuller's prestige and his message drew support for Carey's cause. A motion was passed that "a plan be prepared . . . for propagating the Gospel . . . ."[10] Thus Baptists began their participation in the modern missionary movement.

requires that Christ's churches proclaim the gospel and guide the lost to salvation. Apart from the message of salvation in Christ, there is no answer. Christians and churches must share the message!

Missions/Evangelism Responds Obediently to Christ's Commission (Matthew 28:18-20; John 20:21)

The church must respond to the task of evangelism/missions because this effort is clearly commissed by Christ. After Jesus' resurrection, he commissioned his disciples to proclaim his message to all people. Jesus said he was sending his followers into the world on a redemptive mission as God had sent him (John 20:21). On the mountain in Galilee, the Master set out the Great Commission (Matt. 28:16–20). Jesus' words in the Great Commission contain (1) a great declaration; (2) a great imperative; (3) a great scope; (4) a great methodology; and (5) a great promise.

Jesus' great declaration stated that as risen and glorified Lord, he had received all power or authority in heaven and on earth (28:18). The church never needs to shy away from anything as it carries out the Great Commission, regardless of how difficult it might seem. The church can hold this assurance because the Lord of all authority demands the task and undergirds it! The Commission exists in light of this great declaration that Christ reigns supreme.[5]

The Great Commission contains Jesus' great imperative for witness and disciple-making among all the peoples of the world (Matt. 28:19). The main verb, an imperative, expresses the central command to "make disciples" of all the peoples in the world. Making disciples involves guiding lost souls to faith in Christ, incorporating them into God's family, and helping them to continue to grow in his way of life.

The great scope of the Commission indicates Jesus' desire to reach all the peoples of the world (28:19). Christ commanded that his followers make disciples among "all nations" (28:19), that is, among all the people groups of the world. Reaching every person in all the ethnolinguistic groups (peoples) in the world constitutes the overall purpose and primary command in the Great Commission.[6] The apostle John indicated that in his vision of God's eventual and eternal kingdom, he saw a "great multitude that no one could count, from every nation, tribe and people and language, standing before the throne and in front of the Lamb" (Rev. 7:9; see also 5:9). Here lies the great scope of the Commission.

Note three Greek words Jesus used in Matthew 28:19–20 to enunciate the great methodology for the Commission. These words revealed how the church could make all peoples his disciples. All three of the words are participles. The first Greek word means "going," which, although a participle, has a definite imperative force and can be translated "go." The term indicates that God's people do not have the option of passively sitting and waiting but must be actively and aggressively engaged in missionary effort.

The two other participles—"baptizing" and "teaching"—likewise express means for making disciples (28:19–20). Baptism marks the beginning of the Christian life as the expression of salvation. By baptism, a person proclaims his or her allegiance to Christ and his kingdom. "Teaching them to obey everything I have commanded you" indicates training, not just in doctrine, but in the fullest expression of Christian life and integrity (28:20). The methods set out for the Great Commission include training believers to live out the full measure of what it means to be Christ's person.

The great promise in the Commission assures Christ's followers of his continued presence and power (28:20). The church has the assurance of Christ's presence and power no matter how difficult the task. "No task is too big, no burden too heavy, when Jesus himself is at work in the situation."[7] No place on earth is beyond the reach of God's love in Christ, and no Christian or church is alone while seeking to share the message and make disciples!

The Great Commission contains Christ's command to his people and therefore shows the essential nature of evangelism/mission to the church. Jesus commissions his churches first to mobilization, by going, then to evangelization, by making disciples, on to incorporation, by baptizing, and finally to indoctrination, guiding in Christian living by teaching them to obey all things. The church accepts the Great Commission as essential to its task. Bob Garrett wrote, "The church must take up the Great Commission, not just out of concern for the lost, or pity for those who are needy, but also because ringing in every disciple's ears is the command given by him to whom all authority is given in heaven and earth."[8]

Evangelism/Missions Operates in God's Promise of Divine Power (Acts 1:8)

Christians and churches never seek to carry out the essential task of missions/evangelism in human strength. Evangelism/missions, an essential task of the church, relies on the supernatural power of God for its attainment. Believers and churches feel divine compulsion to evangelize all peoples but never fear having to accomplish the effort apart from divine empowering.

Jesus instructed his disciples in Acts 1:8 that they would be his witnesses in Jerusalem (their immediate context), in Judea (their wider local place), in Samaria (their next neighbor), and then to the ends of the earth (the remotest parts of the world). The disciples were not, however, to become such witnesses until the event by which they would "receive power when the Holy Spirit comes on you" (Acts 1:8). This promised power came upon the disciples on the day of Pentecost (2:1–12).

After the remarkable event of the Spirit's coming upon the believers, many people heard the gospel in words they could fully understand. Upon further hearing the Word of God from Peter, about three thousand people turned in faith to Christ (2:14–41). These believers were then drawn into the Christian fellowship (the church), in which they continued to express their faith in Christ, their unity with one another, and their commitment to the task of evangelism and missions (2:42–47).

Missions/Evangelism—An Essential Task

Missions/evangelism constitutes an essential task of the church that must never be neglected or considered optional. This task is essential because missions/evangelism (1) begins with the loving desire of God for all humankind; (2) meets the ultimate need of people; (3) responds obediently to Christ's commission to his followers; and (4) operates in the promised, supernatural power of God.

Ultimately, missions/evangelism becomes reality as Christians apprehend the awesome desire of God for the salvation of all humankind. May God's people and God's churches be ever faithful to the essential task God has graciously given them.

QUESTIONS

1. The church building had burned, and the members envisioned a difficult time in rebuilding. One member suggested that the money in the missions section of the budget be used locally until the building had been completed. What factors did this member overlook?

2. What assurances does the Bible provide for Christians and churches as they seek to promote evangelism/missions in their communities and in the world?

3. Suggest an outline for a message (lesson, devotional, sermon) on the Great Commission. What points would you want to cover in your presentation?

4. What is the meaning of the concept of proclaiming the gospel of Jesus Christ by word and by deed?

Notes

1. Herschel H. Hobbs, *The Baptist Faith and Message* (Nashville, Tennessee: Convention Press, 1971), 108.
2. Article 11, "The Baptist Faith and Message," 1963.
3. Ebbie C. Smith, "The Call to Missions," *Adult Bible Teacher* (October, November, December 1989): 37.
4. Hobbs, *The Baptist Faith and Message*, 108.
5. Bob Garrett, "The Gospels and Acts: Jesus the Missionary and His Missionary Followers," in *Missiology: An Introduction to the Foundations, History, and Strategies of World Missions*, ed. John Mark Terry, Ebbie Smith, and Justice Anderson (Nashville: Broadman & Holman, 1998), 71.
6. Garrett, *Missiology*, 72.
7. Garrett, *Missiology*, 71.
8. Garrett, *Missiology*, 71.
9. Robert G. Torbet, *A History of the Baptists*, rev. ed. (Valley Forge: The Judson Press, 1963), 80.
10. Torbet, *A History of the Baptists*, 80–82.

Religious Freedom and Separation of Church and State

BACKGROUND SCRIPTURES

Genesis 1:27; 2:7; Matthew 6:6–7, 24; 16:26; 22:15–22; John 8:36; Acts 3:1—4:22; 5:17–29; Romans 6:1–2; 13:1–7; Galatians 5:1, 13; Philippians 3:20; 1 Timothy 2:1–3; James 4:12; 1 Peter 2:12–17; 3:8–17; 4:12–19

FOCAL TEXTS

Matthew 22:15–22; Acts 5:27–29; Romans 13:1–7; 1 Timothy 2:1–3; 1 Peter 2:13–17

MAIN IDEA

"The church should not seek to use the state for its purposes. The state should not commandeer the church for political ends. The state should not favor one religion above another."[1]

STUDY AIM

To summarize biblical teachings on religious liberty and the separation of church and state

QUICK READ

Religious freedom with its corollary of separation of church and state is a precious privilege that was dearly bought by our Baptist forebears and should be cherished and preserved.

The doctrine of religious liberty has been called the distinct contribution that America has made to the science of government. In George W. Truett's historic address, "Baptists and Religious Liberty," he cited the American historian Bancroft as having said, "Freedom of conscience, unlimited freedom of mind, was from the first the trophy of the Baptists."[2] Truett also cited English philosopher John Locke's statement, "The Baptists were the first propounders of absolute liberty, just and true liberty, equal and impartial liberty."[3]

Why did Baptists earnestly contend for the principle of religious freedom? For hundreds of years this small group of often-despised believers endured horrible and heart-breaking persecutions. Baptists saw the terrible results when a government-established church used the civil power to enforce religious edicts. Often Baptists had to stand alone while being persecuted by both Protestant and Catholic governments in Europe and America. If Baptists must stand alone today in defending religious freedom and the separation of the powers of the church and the state, it will not be the first time!

In 1920, George W. Truett could say that Baptists "have never been a party to oppression of conscience."[4] May God grant that it will always be said of the people called Baptists! In his memorable and watershed address on the steps of the U. S. Capitol, Truett went on to make this powerful statement:

> They [Baptists] have forever been the unwavering champions of liberty, both religious and civil. Their contention now is, and has been, and, please God, must ever be, that it is the natural and fundamental and indefeasible right of every human being to worship God or not, according to the dictates of conscience, and, as long as this does not infringe upon the rights of others, they are to be held accountable alone to God for all religious beliefs and practices. . . . It is the consistent and insistent contention of our Baptist people, always and everywhere, that religion must be voluntary and uncoerced, and that it is not the prerogative of any power, whether civil or ecclesiastical to compel men to conform to any religious creed or form of

worship, or to pay taxes for the support of a religious organization to which they do not belong and whose creed they do not believe. God wants free worshipers and no other kind.[5]

The fundamental principles of Baptist theology supporting the doctrine of religious liberty include the following:

1. The Lordship of Jesus Christ over all creation, the church, and the individual lives of Christians

2. The Bible as the only rule of faith and practice, in which the will of Christ is revealed

3. The priesthood of believers (1 Peter 2:9), including individual accountability before God, personal ability to read and interpret Scripture under the guidance of the Holy Spirit, and individual responsibility for witnessing in the name of Jesus Christ, who is the only provision for salvation of the human race

4. The church as a spiritual body with Jesus Christ as Head, the Word of God as the only authority, and with each church member being of equal standing before God

In this Bible study we will examine some of the Scriptural principles that are the foundation for this exceedingly precious Baptist doctrine of religious freedom and the separation of the powers of the church and the state.

The Principle of the Separation of Church and State (Matthew 22:15–22)

Two of the political/religious parties of Jesus' day were the Pharisees and the Herodians. They were rival parties, but they were united in their opposition to Jesus. The Pharisees were very much opposed to the Roman occupation of the Jewish nation. On the other hand, the Herodians were followers of the Herod family, who accommodated themselves to Roman rule.

Apparently the two parties had a running debate on the propriety of paying taxes to Rome. In an attempt to trap Jesus, they brought their dispute to him. With flattering words, they attempted to entice him onto

Matthew 22:15–22 (NASB)

[15]Then the Pharisees went and plotted together how they might trap Him in what He said. [16]And they sent their disciples to Him, along with the Herodians, saying, "Teacher, we know that You are truthful and teach the way of God in truth, and defer to no one; for You are not partial to any. [17]"Tell us then, what do You think? Is it lawful to give a poll-tax to Caesar, or not?" [18]But Jesus perceived their malice, and said, "Why are you testing Me, you hypocrites? [19]"Show Me the coin used for the poll-tax." And they brought Him a denarius. [20]And He said to them, "Whose likeness and inscription is this?" [21]They said to Him, "Caesar's." Then He said to them, "Then render to Caesar the things that are Caesar's; and to God the things that are God's." [22]And hearing this, they were amazed, and leaving Him, they went away.

Acts 5:27–29

[27]When they had brought them, they stood them before the Council. The high priest questioned them, [28]saying, "We gave you strict orders not to continue teaching in this name, and yet, you have filled Jerusalem with your teaching and intend to bring this man's blood upon us." [29]But Peter and the apostles answered, "We must obey God rather than men."

Romans 13:1–7

[1]Every person is to be in subjection to the governing authorities. For there is no authority except from God, and those which exist are established by God. [2]Therefore whoever resists authority has opposed the ordinance of God; and they who have opposed will receive condemnation upon themselves. [3]For rulers are not a cause of fear for good behavior, but for evil. Do you want to have no fear of authority? Do what is good and you will have praise from the same; [4]for it is a minister of God to you for good. But if you do what is evil, be afraid; for it does not bear the sword for nothing; for it is a minister of God, an avenger who brings wrath on the one who practices evil. [5]Therefore it is necessary to be in subjection, not only because of wrath, but also for conscience' sake. [6]For

because of this you also pay taxes, for rulers are servants of God, devoting themselves to this very thing. [7]Render to all what is due them: tax to whom tax is due; custom to whom custom; fear to whom fear; honor to whom honor.

1 Timothy 2:1–3

[1]First of all, then, I urge that entreaties and prayers, petitions and thanksgivings, be made on behalf of all men, [2]for kings and all who are in authority, so that we may lead a tranquil and quiet life in all godliness and dignity. [3]This is good and acceptable in the sight of God our Savior.

1 Peter 2:13–17

[13]Submit yourselves for the Lord's sake to every human institution, whether to a king as the one in authority, [14]or to governors as sent by him for the punishment of evildoers and the praise of those who do right. [15]For such is the will of God that by doing right you may silence the ignorance of foolish men. [16]Act as free men, and do not use your freedom as a covering for evil, but use it as bondslaves of God. [17]Honor all people, love the brotherhood, fear God, honor the king.

the horns of a dilemma. Their question was, "Is it lawful to give tribute unto Caesar, or not?" (Matthew 22:17, KJV).

If Jesus answered "Yes," he would be alienated from the majority of the population. They despised Roman taxes. If he said "No," he could be charged with sedition by the Romans for encouraging the people not to pay their taxes. The Pharisees and the Herodians thought that they had Jesus in an impossible situation, but he confounded their efforts with an object lesson.

Jesus seldom answered questions with a direct "yes" or "no." For example, in this instance, he called for the coin that was used to pay the "tribute," meaning the tax. This Greek word for "tribute" is *kensos*. In Latin the word would be *census*. This "tribute" (KJV) or "poll-tax" (NASB) was an annual tax on every man and woman. The people hated this tax especially. It was very hard on the poor, being a full day's pay for a working man (two days' pay for a married couple). Furthermore, it was seen as a humiliating symbol of Jewish slavery to Rome.

Jesus asked whose image and writing appeared on the coin. The co-conspirators gave the patently obvious answer, "Caesar." They must have been wondering, *Where is he going with this?*

The Struggle for Religious Liberty in New England

Isaac Backus (1724–1806) led the efforts of Baptists in New England to secure religious liberty. One of the examples of persecution cited by Backus involved his own mother. In her own words in a letter, we have a moving description of her experience. By reason of conscience, Mrs. Backus and other members of the church refused to pay the religious tax to support the clergy of the state church, and they were placed in jail.

Norwich, November 4, 1752

Your Brother Samuel lay in prison 20 days. October 15, the collectors came to our house, and took me away to prison about 9:00 o'clock in a dark rainy night. Brothers Hill and Sabin were brought there the next night. We lay in prison 13 days, and then set at liberty by what means I know not. . . . O the condescension of heaven! though I was bound when I was cast into this furnace, yet was I loosed, and found Jesus in the midst of the furnace with me. . . . Now the prison looked like a palace to me. I could bless God for all the laughs and scoffs made at me. . . . Then I could forgive as I would desire to be forgiven, and love my neighbor as myself. . . . These from your loving mother,

ELIZABETH BACKUS[16]

Jesus answered the question so simply that even his enemies marveled at his words. The intended debate ended suddenly, and the inquisitors quietly melted into the astonished crowd.

The answer was a profound and a radically new thought: "Then render to Caesar the things that are Caesar's; and to God the things that are God's" (22:21).

Applications of the Principle (Acts 5:27–29; Romans 13:1–7; 1 Timothy 2:1–3; 1 Peter 2:13–17)

Perhaps Jesus' statement in Matthew 22:21 was the first enunciation of the principle of the separation of civil and spiritual authority. The thought is introduced through the symbolism of two images: the image of Caesar on the coin of the realm and the image of God in the creation of humanity. The applications and ramifications of this revelation are many.

1. God created people, male and female, in his own image. Therefore, humanity has been "endowed with certain 'unalienable' rights," as worded in the Declaration of Independence of the United States. Created in the image of God, each person is of infinite value and worth. Furthermore, each person is answerable only to the Creator in matters of spiritual conscience.

An early English Baptist leader, Thomas Helwys, published a book in 1612 explaining the Baptist position and calling for freedom of religion. Helwys sent an autographed copy to King James I (of "King James Bible" fame) with this inscription, "The King is a mortall man and not God, therefore hath no power over y immortall soules of his subjects to make lawes and ordinances for them and to set spirituall Lords over them."[6] Baptist historian Robert G. Torbet called Helwys' book, "The first claim for freedom of worship to be published in the English language."[7]

For this brave testimony of Baptist convictions, the king had Helwys placed in Newgate prison until his death about 1616.[8] He was but one of thousands who sealed with his life what he had spoken with his lips.

2. The civil government has neither the right nor the capability to legislate or dictate religious doctrine or practice, except in such instances as when other people's freedom is being denied or their safety is being endangered. When both the civil and religious authorities commanded the apostles not to teach in the name of Jesus, "then Peter and the other apostles answered and said, We ought to obey God rather than men" (Acts 5:29, KJV).

Simon Peter proceeded to preach Jesus to the religious council in Jerusalem. When he accused the religious leaders of killing Jesus and hanging him "on a tree" (5:30), the council began to lay plans to kill the apostles also.

Persecution is the ugly fruit that comes from the union of religion and civil government. Even "the land of the free" has a record of religious persecution that is largely unknown. Our remarkable religious heritage must be taught in our Baptist churches if we are to treasure and maintain the religious liberties that have been bought with painful price.

Between 1768 and 1777, no less than thirty Baptist preachers in Virginia were fined, whipped, and imprisoned for nothing more than preaching the gospel and calling for the conversion of sinners. Lewis Craig may have been the first Virginia Baptist preacher to have been indicted in a court of law for public preaching. At his arraignment Craig said, "I thank you, gentlemen of the Grand Jury, for the honor you have done me. While I was wicked and injurious, you took no notice of me; but since I have altered my course of life and endeavored to reform my neighbors, you concern yourselves much about me."[9]

Sitting on that grand jury was John Waller. He was known as "Swearing Jack" before his conversion. As a result of Craig's testimony, Waller soon professed Christ and joined the Baptists. On June 4, 1768, John Waller, Lewis Craig, James Childs, and others were arrested. They were brought before the court and charged as follows: "May it please your worships, these men are great disturbers of the peace; they cannot meet a man upon the road, but they must ram a text of Scripture down his throat."[10]After forty-three days in jail, the prisoners were discharged. However, the persecutors found that the imprisonment of the preachers actually resulted in

The Struggle for Religious Liberty in Virginia

John Leland (1754–1841) led the struggle for religious freedom in Virginia and the South. He is credited with having influenced James Madison to introduce the Bill of Rights as amendments to the Federal Constitution. He wrote the following to answer the question, "Are the rights of conscience alienable, or inalienable?"

. . . Does a man upon entering into social contact surrender his conscience to that society. . . . I judge not, for the following reasons: *First.* Every man must give an account of himself to God, and therefor every man ought to be at liberty to serve God in a way that he can best reconcile to his conscience. *Second.* . . . It would be sinful for a man to surrender that to man, which is to be kept sacred for God. *Third.* But supposing it was right for a man to bind his own conscience, yet surely it is very iniquitous to bind the conscience of his children. . . . *Fourth.* Finally, Religion is a matter between God and individuals; the religious opinions of men not being the objects of civil government, nor in any way under its control.[17]

the furtherance of their cause. They preached regularly through the bars of the jail to larger crowds than they had in their churches.

3. Christians are to obey the law of government (Romans 13:1–7). Consider what these verses tell us about church and state and their relationship.

- Government authority is ordained by God (13:1).
- To resist government authority is to resist the ordinance of God (13:2), unless the will of God and government are in opposition (Acts 5:29).
- Government should restrain evil and promote good (Rom.13:3).
- Government should administer temporal justice (13:4; see 1 Peter 2:14).
- Christians should pay taxes for the support of civil government (Rom. 13:6).

- Christians should pay proper respect to government authority (13:7).

Other New Testament Scriptures provide additional insights.

- Christians should pray for the leaders of government (1 Timothy 2:1–2).
- Government should promote domestic tranquility (2:2).
- Good citizenship pleases God (2:3).
- Christians are to submit themselves "to every ordinance of man for the Lord's sake" (1 Peter 2:13, KJV).
- Good citizenship bears a positive witness before the world (2:15).
- Christians should exercise liberty as servants of God and not as an excuse for evil (2:16).

4. The power of the civil government to tax should not be used to support religion or religious institutions. The Bible teaches that church ministries ought to be supported by the voluntary offerings of its adherents and sympathizers. God desires a willing heart. "Take ye from among you an offering unto the Lord: whosoever is of a willing heart, let him bring it" (Exodus 35:5, KJV). "Each one must do just as he has purposed in his heart, not grudgingly or under compulsion, for God loves a cheerful giver" (2 Corinthians 9:7).

When it was proposed to the Virginia legislature in colonial times that government money should be used to support the teachers of the Christian religion, James Madison led the opposition. He said, " . . . The Christian religion itself . . . disavows a dependence on the powers of this world . . . this religion both existed and flourished, not only without the support of human laws, but in spite of every opposition from them."[11]

Benjamin Franklin wrote in a letter, "When a religion is good, I can see that it will support itself; and when it cannot support itself, and God does not take care to support it, so that its professors are obliged to call for the help of the civil power, it is a sign, I apprehend, of its being a bad one."[12]

5. All people should be free to worship God according to the directions of their own conscience and to practice and propagate their religious convictions. We do

The Struggle for Religious Liberty in Texas

One reason Texas Baptists have always been strong advocates of religious freedom and the separation of church and state is because Texas was once under the domination of a state-supported church. When Moses Austin asked to be allowed to settle 300 families in Texas in 1820, all colonists were required to be Roman Catholics or agree to convert to that church before they could settle. Even after the Mexican Revolution of 1820 achieved independence from Spain, the Roman Catholic Church continued as the official state religion. Only priests were allowed to conduct funerals or perform weddings.

Joseph L. Bays, Kentucky Baptist preacher and friend of Daniel Boone, joined the colonists of Moses and Stephen F. Austin. Bays preached his first sermon in Texas in 1820 at the cabin of Joseph Hinds, about eighteen miles from San Augustine. The Bays family became a part of the original 300 settlers of the Austin colony.

Bays was arrested in 1823 while preaching in San Felipe. While he was being taken to San Antonio for trial, Bays overcame his guard and escaped. He later went to San Antonio, not to stand trial, but to preach. Bays became a close friend of Sam Houston and fought in the Battle of San Jacinto in 1836.[18]

well to remember that on spiritual matters, each of us is accountable to God (Rom. 14:12).

Indeed, Christians are advised to examine themselves to see whether they be in the faith and to prove for themselves that the Lord Jesus Christ is within them (2 Cor. 13:5). In the practice of religious life, neither Daniel nor his fellow Hebrews would be governed by the authority of a temporal king. As a result Daniel was cast into the lions' den, and Shadrach, Meshach, and Abed-nego were cast into a fiery furnace (Daniel 6:16; 3:14–18).

In 1651 pastor John Clarke, along with two Baptist laymen, Obadiah Holmes and John Randell, went up from Newport, Rhode Island, to

Lynn, Massachusetts, to visit an aged and blind Baptist friend, William Witters. It took two days to walk the eighty miles. On Sunday they held a private religious service in Witters' home. In the midst of the service two constables broke into the house and arrested the three visitors in the act of worship. This was a serious offence. It was a violation of the law for anyone to hold divine services without the consent of the government-established Congregational Church of the Massachusetts Bay Colony.

At their trial, they were accused, among other things, that they did "Baptize such as were Baptized before . . . And also did deny the lawfull-ness of Baptizing of Infants."[13] Puritan John Cotton, determined to have a theocratic state, accused the three of being soul murderers because they denied the saving power of infant baptism.

The three men were given the choice of a whipping or a fine. The fines of two of the men were paid, but Obadiah Holmes refused to allow his fine to be paid. After several weeks in jail, Holmes was taken to Boston Commons where his hands were tied to a stake. He was stripped to the waist, and the flogger used a whip of three hard leather lashes, stopping three times to spit on his hands, and laying on the whip with all his might.[14]

During the whipping Holmes prayed that the Lord would not lay this sin to their charge. He continued to preach all the way through the

Texas' Declaration of Independence

Richard Ellis, a Baptist, presided at the convention when Texas declared independence on March 2, 1836, and again on March 17 when the first Texas constitution was adopted. Baptist historian Robert A. Baker writes,

> One of the injustices named by the Convention as the basis for the Declaration reads as follows: "It denies us the right of worshiping the Allmighty (sic) according to the dictates of our own conscience, by the support of a national religion calculated to promote the temporal interests of its human functionaries rather than the glory of the true and living God."[19]

Wisdom on Church and State

"Neither church nor state should exercise authority over the other. History records that a free church in a free state proves a blessing to both."[20]

punishment. When the ordeal was over, he said to the magistrates, "You have struck me as with roses."[15] Holmes was so injured by the severity of the whipping that he was unable to leave Boston for several weeks. He could rest at night only by crouching on his elbows and knees. He carried the scars of the beating to his grave as a badge of honor for his devotion.

Preserving Religious Freedom

Religious freedom is a right that was achieved only after years of struggle. It cost our Baptist forebears persecution, whippings, imprisonment, sufferings, and painful horrible death.

No matter what course others may take, we should preserve the right to witness to the saving grace of Jesus Christ our Savior and to worship him according to the pattern of Scripture. We should not use the sword of secular power in spiritual matters. Rather we should use the sword of the Spirit only. We should not coerce any person to conform to religion. We should protect the religious freedom of minorities since we were once a despised and persecuted sect. In most of the world today, Baptists are still a small minority, and we must hold these principles dear for their sakes also.

QUESTIONS

1. What are four fundamental principles of religious freedom?

2. What difficult issues regarding religious liberty do we face today?

3. How can Baptists respond to challenges to religious liberty in light of biblical teachings?

4. Why should Christians exercise good citizenship?

Notes

1. Herschel H. Hobbs, *The Baptist Faith and Message* (Nashville, Tennessee: Convention Press, 1971), 142.
2. George W. Truett in an address made on May 16, 1920, on the steps of the U. S. Capitol Building. The full text of George W. Truett's sermon, "Baptists and Religious Liberty," can be accessed on the internet at this address: http://www.bjcpa.org/pubs/fultruet.html
3. Truett, "Baptists and Religious Liberty," 1920.
4. Truett, "Baptists and Religious Liberty," 1920.
5. Truett, "Baptists and Religious Liberty," 1920.
6. Cited in Robert G. Torbet, *A History of the Baptists*, rev. ed. (Philadelphia: The Judson Press, 1963), 38.
7. Torbet, *A History of the Baptists*, 38. Thomas Helwys' book was titled *A Short Declaration of the Mystery of Iniquity*.
8. Torbet, *A History of the Baptists*, 39.
9. Harry Leon McBeth, *The Baptist Heritage* (Nashville, Tennessee: Broadman Press, 1987), 270.
10. McBeth, *A Source Book for Baptist Heritage* (Nashville, Tennessee: Broadman Press, 1990), 183.
11. A. P. Stokes and L. Pfeffer, *Church and State in the United States* (New York: Kohn, Harper and Row Publishers, 1964), 57
12. Stokes and Pfeffer, *Church and State in the United States*, 41.
13. McBeth, *A Source Book for Baptist Heritage*, 93.
14. O. K. Armstrong & M. M. Armstrong, *The Indomitable Baptists* (Garden City, N.J.: Doubleday and Company, Inc., 1967), 60–62.
15. McBeth, *The Baptist Heritage*, 140.
16. McBeth, *A Source Book for Baptist Heritage*, 173.
17. McBeth, *A Source Book for Baptist Heritage*, 179.
18. McBeth, Texas Baptists: *A Sesquicentennial History* (Dallas, Texas: BAPTISTWAY PRESS®, 1998), 14.
19. Robert A. Baker, *The Blossoming Desert* (Waco, Texas: Word Books, 1970), 23.
20. Hobbs, *The Baptist Faith and Message*, 143.

Salvation Only by Grace Through Faith

BACKGROUND SCRIPTURES

Exodus 6:2–8; Matthew 1:21; 4:17; 16:21–26; Luke 1:68–69; 2:28–32; John 1:11–14,29; 3:3–21,36; 5:24; 10:9; Acts 2:21; 4:12; 15:11; 16:25–34; 20:32; Romans 1:16–18; 3:23–25; 4:3–13; 5:8–10; 10:9–13; Galatians 2:20; 3:13; 6:15; Ephesians 1:7; 2:8–22; Hebrews 5:8–9; 9:24–28; 1 John 2:1–2; Revelation 3:20

FOCAL TEXTS

Acts 16:25–34; Romans 1:16–18; Galatians 2:20; Ephesians 2:8–10

MAIN IDEA

"Salvation by grace means salvation as a free gift on God's part. . . . Receiving salvation as an unmerited gift on God's part is faith."[1]

STUDY AIM

To explain the way of salvation

QUICK READ

Two facets of God's grace are the grace of salvation and the grace of daily living. God saves us, not just from hell, but *to* a specific lifestyle.

Sunday as I looked at the folks in my Sunday School class, my fellow choir members, and the congregation of friends, I understood God's grace in a new way. Yes, God saves us from sin and hell, but God also saves us to be the Lord's children, part of the community of faith. Salvation is by grace through faith; we cannot earn salvation or membership in the body of believers. God's grace, the "unearned merit," reaches into our lives, establishes an eternal, life-saving relationship between ourselves and God, and grafts us into the body of Christ. We thus are God's children in a family, not orphans left alone to make our way through the world. God performs this miracle in our lives without coercion of any type. The Lord requires only our faith.

Midnight Salvation (Acts 16:25–34)

As a child, I liked the story of the Philippian jailer (Acts 16:25–34). As an adult, I marvel at the powerful way God saved the jailer and affirmed the work of Paul and Silas. What a scene! Midnight, a stinking jail cell, stinging whip marks, and two men singing!

The Philippian officials jailed Paul and Silas because of false accusations, beat them without a hearing, and consigned them to the care of the jailer (see 16:16–24). The jailer understood these men needed special guarding. So he placed them in the most interior, lightless, and well-guarded cell in the prison. Chained to stocks, Paul and Silas had no way to escape. The jailer made sure these prisoners were secure because if they escaped he would be executed in their stead. This is the scene from which God's grace would pour into the lives of the jailer and his household.

In the face of possible death, Paul and Silas sang and prayed. At a time when I would have curled up in the fetal position and withdrawn, these two missionaries continued in strong fellowship with God. What faith! Both had experienced the grace of God. God had saved Paul, a persecutor and hater of the church, in a spectacular manner on the road to Damascus (9:1–30). Silas was a leader of the Jerusalem church (15:22).

Acts 16:25–34 (NRSV)

[25]About midnight Paul and Silas were praying and singing hymns to God, and the prisoners were listening to them. [26]Suddenly there was an earthquake, so violent that the foundations of the prison were shaken; and immediately all the doors were opened and everyone's chains were unfastened. [27]When the jailer woke up and saw the prison doors wide open, he drew his sword and was about to kill himself, since he supposed that the prisoners had escaped. [28]But Paul shouted in a loud voice, "Do not harm yourself, for we are all here." [29]The jailer called for lights, and rushing in, he fell down trembling before Paul and Silas. [30]Then he brought them outside and said, "Sirs, what must I do to be saved?" [31]They answered, "Believe on the Lord Jesus, and you will be saved, you and your household." [32]They spoke the word of the Lord to him and to all who were in his house. [33]At the same hour of the night he took them and washed their wounds; then he and his entire family were baptized without delay. [34]He brought them up into the house and set food before them; and he and his entire household rejoiced that he had become a believer in God.

Romans 1:16–18

[16]For I am not ashamed of the gospel; it is the power of God for salvation to everyone who has faith, to the Jew first and also to the Greek. [17]For in it the righteousness of God is revealed through faith for faith; as it is written, "The one who is righteous will live by faith."

[18]For the wrath of God is revealed from heaven against all ungodliness and wickedness of those who by their wickedness suppress the truth.

Galatians 2:20

. . . It is no longer I who live, but it is Christ who lives in me. And the life I now live in the flesh I live by faith in the Son of God, who loved me and gave himself for me.

Although in pain and facing an uncertain future, Paul and Silas knew God worked in every trial. Thus they responded with hymns and prayer. Perhaps they sang the first-century equivalent of "Amazing Grace" and prayed that God's will be done. In the face of adversity, God's grace enabled them to live in the moment and to believe God's presence would sustain them. Supporting each other, they presented Christ to their fellow inmates.

The jailer finished his duties and went to bed, leaving the prisoners to their fears and dark thoughts. But as Paul and Silas prayed, sang, and witnessed for the Lord, the felons surrounding them listened. I have a mental image of prisoners straining against cell bars to hear more clearly what these two men said and sang. Through the murk of the prison came sounds of hope, peace, and promise—sounds the felons hadn't heard for many years or perhaps had never heard. The faithfulness of Paul and Silas communicated hope to the hopeless in that dank place.

How do you and I react in times of uncertainty and pain? Do we go to God or withdraw from God?

God's love and grace don't depend on our circumstances. They are constant in our lives. The *Baptist Faith and Message* of 1963 uses the terms "regeneration," "sanctification," and "glorification" to explain the process of salvation (Article 4). As stated in an old adage, we have been saved from the punishment of sin (regeneration), we are being saved from the power of sin (sanctification), and we will be saved from the presence of

Ephesians 2:8–10

[8]For by grace you have been saved through faith, and this is not your own doing; it is the gift of God—[9]not the result of works, so that no one may boast. [10]For we are what he has made us, created in Christ Jesus for good works, which God prepared beforehand to be our way of life.

sin (glorification). God implants saving grace in our souls when we become believers. How we respond to that grace in times of trial says more about us than about God. Paul and Silas responded with faith and courage.

God sometimes uses spectacular means to get our attention. In the case of the Philippian jailer, an earthquake hit the jail to grab his attention. At midnight, when the jailer slept soundly and God's followers sang hymns, an earthquake shook the chains from the prisoners, swung open cell doors, and freed the felons. Awakened, the jailer ran to check his wards. He assumed they had fled the prison. Losing prisoners, especially two such important ones as Paul and Silas, would have meant the jailer's death. Rather than face public execution, he decided to commit suicide. Before he could, Paul called to him. A word of salvation, of hope, came out of the darkness. What an unexpected reprieve from death!

The jailer immediately wanted what made these two men different, what gave them the courage to sing, to pray, and to stay when they had the chance to flee. Quietly and simply, Paul told the jailer, "'Believe on the Lord Jesus'" (16:31). Paul created no requirements before salvation. He did not require the jailer to stop sacrificing to idols before salvation, and he did not question the jailer about his political or moral views on critical issues of the day before extending God's grace. The only act on the jailer's part in the process of salvation was to believe in the Lord Jesus. So simple but so profound.

Paul also made a promise to the jailer (see 16:31). If you believe, your household will be influenced, too. Community comes with belief. A life-changing event affects those close to the person saved, and God's grace flows through believers into the aching hearts of the lost. Without hesitation, the jailer accepted God's grace and took Paul and Silas to his home for medical attention. While there, the two men continued their task of witnessing, and the jailer's household came to the Lord. From the grace of God and the faithfulness of two prisoners, a new community of faith emerged.

"'Believe on the Lord Jesus, and you will be saved, you and your household'" (16:31). Such a plain, straightforward way of introducing someone to God. No frills, no barriers, just faith.

What barriers do we put in the way of people seeking the Lord? What barriers do we place in our own path as we seek to follow Christ? One thing we can know with certainty—God's grace surmounts and destroys all barriers.

A Tower Experience (Romans 1:16–18)

Martin Luther (1483–1546) found no peace, no matter how many hours he spent in confession, no matter how much he beat himself, no matter how strongly he longed for relationship with God. Even as a monk and a priest, peace eluded Luther's grasp. He yearned for acceptance by God. One day, as he sat in a tower room preparing a seminary lecture on Romans 1:16–18, the gospel smacked him right between the eyes. God transferred Luther's focus from the wrath of God consuming all sinners to God's grace saving through faith.

The Protestant Reformation latched onto this insight, and as Baptists developed in the early 1600s, they affirmed Luther's emphasis that salvation is *sola gratias*—solely of grace. We don't gain salvation by being baptized as infants or by being born in America. We don't earn salvation by growing up in a Baptist church or by going to a Baptist school. The true gospel "is the power of God for salvation to everyone who has faith . . . " (Romans 1:16). Salvation comes by the Lord's grace to those who believe.

In our age of tolerance, we easily forget that people need God's grace. Romans 1:18 reminds us that God's wrath is real. People need to know that eternal consequences flow from their actions and attitudes. We ignore opportunities to share the gospel because we don't want to be labeled as fanatics. We remain silent in the face of

Lottie Moon

Lottie Moon lived the gospel daily. Although she made mistakes like all of us, she modeled Christ's love to the Chinese with whom she worked. Adopting their dress, eating their food, and mastering their language, she became a "little Christ" for the people of Ping Tu for several decades. God's grace poured into folks in Ping Tu because Lottie Moon accepted God's power to live a Christian life, and because they responded in faith to the gospel. Illness plagued her. Fatigue made her feel inadequate for the task. The lack of trained missionary personnel made her work overwhelming. Yet, in it all, she persevered in sharing the gospel by word and deed.

Unable to address men directly because of cultural norms, when she spoke to women inside a house, she raised her voice and articulated each word so that the men gathered outside near the windows heard the gospel clearly. From baking cookies for the town's children, to offering aid to the poor and spiritual guidance to new Christians, Charlotte Diggs Moon lived the gospel, a life of good works.

immorality or sin because we don't want to appear judgmental. We cling to the gift of God's grace for ourselves, hope others find it, too, and yet do little to share that word of grace. How sad. Luther's insight caused him to explode into his religious world with the radical claim that God's grace is sufficient. What will our insight into God's grace cause us to do?

God reminds us of Paul and Silas in prison, and God will grant us the courage to explain the gospel to a person in spiritual need. As we live in God's grace, the Lord guides us to take loving stands on important moral issues in our world. By ones and twos, by families and congregations, we can make a difference in the spiritual and moral lives of those around us. As members of the body of Christ, we gain strength to accomplish godly purposes, and wisdom to live as Christians. But we must be willing to share God's simple message—"'Believe on the Lord Jesus'" (Acts 16:31).

God's Grace in Daily Life
(Galatians 2:20; Ephesians 2:8–10)

From the early 1600s when Baptists began writing confessions of faith to let the world know what a particular community of faith believed, Baptists have asserted that salvation comes by grace through faith. This idea shaped the Baptist understanding of baptism, the Lord's Supper, the function of the church, and the need to share the gospel. Salvation by grace defines who we are as Baptists.

God lays claim to our lives. In Galatians 2:20, Paul explained the place of the Lord's grace in our lives: ". . . it is no longer I who live, but it is Christ who lives in me. And the life I now live in the flesh I live by faith in the Son of God, who loved me and gave himself for me." If we take this doctrine seriously, we should live our lives as "little Christs" wherever we are. "Christ in us" means we share our knowledge of God's gift of salvation with a world that desperately needs that knowledge. We cannot create faith, and we cannot create grace. We can, however, create an understanding of God's desire for relationship with those we know, and we can live out God's grace in our world. The Baptist doctrine of salvation by grace through faith means we share the gospel each moment by how we live, how we present "Christ in us." Let us live a deliberate, consistent, and grace-filled gospel before the world.

God's gracious gift of salvation is free, but it is also costly! Christ demands our all. As we come to the Lord, we live daily in faith. Too, as God's grace embraces our lives, we embrace our world with faith, love, and grace. In a real sense, we are pathways for God's grace into the world. We extend God's promises to people who need those promises. Christ

Living a "Christ" Life

1. Set aside a time each day to spend at least ten minutes in prayer.
2. Ask God to guide each decision you make, each word you speak, and each gesture you make during the day.
3. Be silent for five minutes, allowing God time to speak to you.
4. As you face tough situations during the day, silently ask for God's grace to surround the issue.
5. Before going to bed, thank God for evidence of God's grace during the day.

lives in us to sustain us and through us to sustain the world. What a wonderful way to experience God!

In Ephesians 2:8–10, Paul reminds us that salvation is God's grace-gift. Verse 10 also reminds us that this gift lays claim to our lives. God calls us to live godly lives. Salvation, as we already have noted, is a process that includes regeneration (saved), sanctification (being saved), and glorification (will be saved). The words in parentheses in the previous sentence refer to what we might call the "tenses" of the Christian life. Regeneration speaks of *having been saved*, sanctification of *being saved*, and glorification of *will be saved*, referring to the fullness of salvation that is yet to come. Walking with God daily is as much a grace-gift part of salvation as being saved from eternal damnation. In some ways, we find it more difficult to live a godly life than to accept Christ by faith. Sharing our faith and living as God would have us to live come as part of the process, however. Do we take the "daily" part of salvation seriously enough?

Baptists take the gospel very seriously. As stated by Paul in Romans 1:18, the unworthy will fall under God's wrath, and we believe all humans fit that description. Without Christ, no one can be a child of God or accept God's grace. We support missions and evangelism to bring the knowledge of Christ to the world. Yet, we find it easier to give money to missions or to pay a preacher than to live a Christian life that presents the gospel to the world, in word and deed.

"For we are what he [God] has made us, created in Christ Jesus for good works, which God prepared beforehand to be our way of life" (Eph. 2:10). "Our way of life" is to do "good works." What a challenge! Being Christ in the world is a difficult task. But Paul assured us, from his life story and from his writing, that God's grace proves sufficient for our daily lives. When was the last time we began our days with a "thank you" for the grace to get through the next twenty-four hours as a "little Christ" in the world? How often do we experience God's power in daily life? What effort do we put forth to live out our faith in God's grace through our personal relationships, within our families, and in our work habits?

Paul promised us, and as Baptists we take this promise seriously, that God intends us to walk with the Lord each moment. Stumbling over spiritual obstacles, erecting ungodly barriers, we forget that the Lord knows what we face and provides more than enough grace to meet our needs.

God made us for good works, to be "little Christs" in the world, and told us exactly what doing good works means. (See Romans 12:1–2, for example.) We need to participate deliberately in God's plan each day. Saved from the punishment of sin, we must live saved from the power of sin, and we will be saved from the presence of sin. The gospel is the message we are to share with the world.

Too, we are to live our daily lives as members of a community of faith, accountable to one another and to God for our attitudes, beliefs, and lives. By accepting wise counsel, godly advice, and loving inspiration, we benefit from God's grace. The promise of salvation includes membership in a church family. God provides a community of believers to provide encouragement, to help us make tough decisions, and to enable us to work through grief and distress. We struggle side-by-side with other Christians, learning how to be God's children and how to share that knowledge with the world. As Baptists, we believe that God's grace empowers us to live Christ-like lives, supported by a community of faith. Praise God, from whom all blessings flow!

QUESTIONS

1. When did you last share the gospel verbally? How did it feel?

2. Within you, what barriers exist to sharing the gospel with co-workers or family?

3. How might God overcome those barriers?

4. Looking at the last year, what experiences of God's grace can you point to?

5. Who in your church shared God's grace with you?

6. With whom have you shared God's grace?

Notes

1. Walter Thomas Conner, *Christian Doctrine* (Nashville, Tennessee: Broadman Press, 1937), 197.

The Security
of the Believer

BACKGROUND SCRIPTURES

John 5:24; 10:27–30; 17:6, 12, 17–18; Acts 20:32; Romans
5:9–10; 8:28–39; Ephesians 1:4–23; 2:1–10; Colossians
1:12–14; 2 Thessalonians 2:13–15; 2 Timothy 1:12; 2:19;
1 Peter 1:2–5, 13; 2:4–10; 1 John 3:2

FOCAL TEXTS

John 10:27–29; Romans 8:31–39; 1 Peter 1:3–5

MAIN IDEA

"One who is truly regenerated will continue in faith and will be
finally delivered from sin."[1]

STUDY AIM

To summarize the New Testament teachings on Christian
perseverance and its implications for their lives

QUICK READ

Believers are saved by the grace of God and kept by the power
of God.

The eternal security of the believer in Christ is one of the great doctrines in the Bible, but it also is one of the least understood. Of all Baptist beliefs this is probably the most controversial. After almost fifty years in the ministry, I have heard more people say that they could never become Baptists because of this one belief than any other teaching. This doctrine is also known as "the perseverance of the saints," or more popularly it is stated as "once saved, always saved."

Why do so many people find this doctrine difficult to understand or accept? Sincere people raise questions like the following: *What about those who were once professing believers but now are living wicked, ungodly lives? Wouldn't that doctrine be an encouragement to sin? Besides, doesn't it say somewhere in the Bible that you have to work out your own salvation and that you can fall from grace?*

Such objections deserve serious consideration, but first let's look at the teachings of Scripture on the subject. Then we will attempt to answer the objections.

Biblical Evidence for Eternal Security

John 10:27–29 gives three very important facts about the eternal security of the believer in Christ.

1. His Sheep Are a Purchased Possession (John 10:27).

Jesus used the sheep/shepherd analogy to teach that sheep belong to and are purchased by the shepherd. No flock of sheep ever got together and pooled their wool into a mutual fund to purchase a shepherd. Rather the shepherd always purchases the sheep. Jesus said, "I am the good shepherd: the good shepherd giveth his life for the sheep," (10:11, KJV). Again, "I lay down My life for the sheep" (10:15). Pastors are urged "to feed the church of God, which he hath purchased with his own blood" (Acts 20:28, KJV).

It would be a mistake to believe that Christians are purchasing a Savior on the installment plan, and that salvation will be repossessed if the weekly

John 10:27–29 (NASB)

27"My sheep hear My voice, and I know them, and they follow Me; 28and I give eternal life to them, and they will never perish; and no one will snatch them out of My hand. 29"My Father, who has given them to Me, is greater than all; and no one is able to snatch them out of the Father's hand."

Romans 8:31–39

31What then shall we say to these things? If God is for us, who is against us? 32He who did not spare His own Son, but delivered Him over for us all, how will He not also with Him freely give us all things? 33Who will bring a charge against God's elect? God is the one who justifies; 34who is the one who condemns? Christ Jesus is He who died, yes, rather who was raised, who is at the right hand of God, who also intercedes for us. 35Who will separate us from the love of Christ? Will tribulation, or distress, or persecution, or famine, or nakedness, or peril, or sword? 36Just as it is written,

"FOR YOUR SAKE WE ARE BEING PUT TO DEATH ALL DAY LONG;

WE WERE CONSIDERED AS SHEEP TO BE SLAUGHTERED."

37But in all these things we overwhelmingly conquer through Him who loved us. 38For I am convinced that neither death, nor life, nor angels, nor principalities, nor things present, nor things to come, nor powers, 39nor height, nor depth, nor any other created thing, will be able to separate us from the love of God, which is in Christ Jesus our Lord.

1 Peter 1:3–5

3Blessed be the God and Father of our Lord Jesus Christ, who according to His great mercy has caused us to be born again to a living hope through the resurrection of Jesus Christ from the dead, 4to obtain an inheritance which is imperishable and undefiled and will not fade away, reserved in heaven for you, 5who are protected by the power of God through faith for a salvation ready to be revealed in the last time.

payments are not made. Christians are not purchasing Christ, but he has already purchased us. A proof that the sheep have been purchased by the Shepherd is that they hear his voice and are following him (John 10:27).

2. His Sheep Receive Eternal Life As a Gift (John 10:28).

The Good Shepherd said, "I give unto them eternal life . . . " (10:28, KJV). Eternal life is a gift from God. It is not of works lest any person should boast (see Ephesians 2:8–9).

One of the most basic of all biblical doctrines is that salvation comes by the grace of God and not by the work of human beings. If it were possible, what could cause people to lose eternal life after they had received it? The only reason would be that they failed to maintain their good works. If that were true, then salvation would depend on their good works.

The Bible clearly states, "I do not frustrate the grace of God: for if righteousness come by the law, then Christ is dead in vain" (Galatians 2:21, KJV).

"I Don't Know Whether I Am Saved or Not"

Across the years, many people have said to me, "I don't whether I am saved or not." I have always said to them that the matter can be settled if in repentance and faith they will call on the name of the Lord. I suggest that they pray something like this, *Lord, I don't know whether I was saved before or not, but I do know that I want to give my life to you now. Please forgive me, and I am giving you my whole life.* Then I suggest, "You live with that decision for a little while. You may realize that you really were a Christian but lacked assurance. If you decide that this is the first time that you have really given your life to Christ, then you need to confess him publicly and follow him in believer's baptism." It is a sobering fact that most of the people who prayed under those conditions, later came to be baptized. We certainly ought to examine our hearts to see whether we are in the faith (2 Corinthians 13:5).

If we attempt to substitute our works for his grace, then we are frustrating the grace that God desires to give us. If we could be saved by keeping the works of the law, there would be no reason for Christ to have died upon the cross. If there were any other way for the human race to be redeemed, Christ would not have suffered and died for our sins. The doctrine of eternal security is inseparably related to the basic biblical doctrine of salvation by grace. You can't have one without the other.

But some have said, *It will take all that God and I can do together to get me to heaven. It will take both grace and works.* This feeling is not uncommon, but the Bible clearly states that grace and works cannot be mixed to produce salvation. "And if by grace, then is it no more of works: otherwise grace is no more grace. But if it be of works, then is it no more grace: otherwise work is no more work" (Romans 11:6, KJV). Salvation is either a gift of grace or a product of our works. It cannot be both. Salvation is a gift of grace.

3. His Sheep Are Kept by the Power of God (John 10:28–29).

The Lord Jesus said, "No one will snatch them out of My hand" (10:28). He also said, "No one is able to snatch them out of the Father's hand" (10:29). Furthermore, Scripture states, "Ye were sealed with that holy Spirit of promise" (Eph. 1:13, KJV). So the Bible teaches that the sheep are kept by the power of the Son and of the Father and are sealed by the Holy Spirit. Believers are not kept by their own strength, but by the power of the triune God.

This emphasis was also the personal testimony of Paul when he wrote to Timothy, "For I know whom I have believed, and am persuaded that he is able to keep that which I have committed unto him against that day" (2 Timothy 1:12, KJV). Paul did not say, *I am able to keep that which I have committed unto him.* He clearly understood that *Christ* is able to keep us.

Simon Peter also gave the same testimony concerning the incorruptible inheritance that is reserved in heaven for us, "Who are kept by the power of God through faith unto salvation ready to be revealed in the last time" (1 Peter 1:5, KJV). Peter also declared that we are kept by the power of God and not by our own will power.

Perhaps the most emphatic statement of the eternal security of the believer is recorded in Romans 8:31–39. The passage closes with these powerful words of comfort and confidence. "For I am persuaded, that neither death, nor life, nor angels, nor principalities, nor powers, nor things present, nor things to come. Nor height, nor depth, nor any other creature, shall be able to separate us from the love of God, which is in Christ Jesus our Lord" (Rom. 8:38–39, KJV)

Objections to the Doctrine of Eternal Security

Objections to the doctrine of eternal security should receive serious consideration. Here are some objections that people sometimes make.

First, someone may ask, *What about the people who confessed Christ but now are living wicked and ungodly lives? Do you mean that they are assured of heaven even though they have renounced their faith?* No, of course not. Receiving Christ is such a life-changing experience that it is called being "born again" (John 3:3). If there is no evidence of a new nature, no likeness to a new Father, no fruit of the Spirit evidenced, then there is scant reason to believe that the person was ever saved.

The Lord Jesus himself warned, "Not everyone that saith unto me, Lord, Lord, shall enter into the kingdom of heaven; but he that doeth the will of my Father which is in heaven. Many will say to me in that day, Lord, Lord, have we not prophesied in thy name? and in thy name have cast out devils? and in thy name done many wonderful works? And then will I profess unto them, I never knew you: depart from me, ye that work iniquity" (Matthew 7:21–23, KJV). Notice that the Lord did not say that he once knew them and now does not, but he said, "I never knew you . . . " in spite of all their professed religious works.

The Bible teaches that apparent "departure from the faith" is evidence of never having been in the faith. "They went out from us, but they were

Think About It

If people could be lost after they have been saved, how many sins would they have to commit or how many works must they fail to do in order to lose salvation? Are all the good works to be added to one side of the scale to be counterbalanced by the evil works on the other side? If that were true, then we would not need a Savior. We could save ourselves.

No system of justice works that way. We are not allowed to break the law as many times as we have kept the law before we can be prosecuted. If you have stopped at the stop sign a thousand times, are you allowed to run through the stop sign a thousand times before you receive a traffic citation?

not of us; for if they had been of us, they would no doubt have continued with us: but they went out, that they might be made manifest that they were not all of us" (1 John 2:19, KJV).

It is possible, however, for Christians to be "backslidden" and out of fellowship with God. While we can never lose our relationship with God as Father when we have been born again, we can be out of fellowship with him. Every true child of God desires to have fellowship with the Father in heaven. When the fellowship is broken, it can be restored when we confess our sins and return to the Father (see 1 John 1:7–9).

Simon Peter was backslidden when he denied the Lord, but this disruption of fellowship did not last long. Simon Peter was at the empty tomb and in the upper room on resurrection day. Judas, however, was never a child of God. The Lord Jesus knew this all along. He said to the Twelve, "One of you is a devil" (John 6:70). It was the devil that put into the heart of Judas to betray Jesus. Judas was never truly saved.

We should not give false assurance to anyone that they have received eternal life on the basis of a childhood experience or church membership when there is no evidence of the fruit of salvation.

Consider a second objection: *Wouldn't the doctrine of eternal security of the believer be an encouragement to sin? If I believed in "once saved always saved," then I would go out and sin all I want to.* If this doctrine seems an encouragement to people to sin, then they have misunderstood its meaning. If we have truly been saved, then our natures have been changed, and it grieves us when we sin and fall short of the glory of God.

The doctrine of the eternal security of the believer is no excuse for living contentedly in sin. If people can live wickedly all during the week and then show up in church on Sunday and be perfectly contented in the worship of a holy God, then they should surely examine themselves to see if they are truly in the faith.

A third question may be asked: *But what about the verse that says, "Work out your own salvation." Doesn't that mean that we must continue to work for our salvation?*

That verse is found in Philippians 2:12: "Wherefore, my beloved, as ye have always obeyed, not as in my presence only, but now much more in my absence, work our your own salvation with fear and trembling" (KJV).

One of the important principles of biblical interpretation is to examine the context in which a verse is found. Otherwise, some strange doctrines have been concocted by stringing isolated verses together. The very next

Kept by the Power of God

All true believers endure to the end. Those whom God has accepted in Christ, and sanctified by His Spirit, will never fall away from the state of grace, but shall persevere to the end. Believers may fall into sin through neglect and temptation, whereby they grieve the Spirit, impair their graces and comforts, bring reproach on the cause of Christ, and temporal judgments on themselves, yet they shall be kept by the power of God through faith unto salvation.

—ARTICLE 5, "THE BAPTIST FAITH AND MESSAGE," 1963

verse explains, "For it is God which worketh in you both to will and to do of his good pleasure" (Phil. 2:13, KJV). It is God who is working in us, and we are not earning our salvation by our good works.

A fourth objection comes in a question like this: *Isn't there a verse that says you can "fall from grace"?* A verse containing that thought is found in the Book of Galatians. Remember first that Galatians was written for the purpose of teaching that salvation comes by God's grace and not by our works. The entire verse reads like this: "Christ is become of no effect unto you, whosoever of you are justified by the law; ye are fallen from grace" (Galatians 5:4, KJV).

"Fallen from grace" does not mean that they had lost their salvation. Paul wrote to the Galatians as believers and repeatedly called them "brethren" (for examples, see 4:32, immediately before this passage, and 5:11, immediately after). In Galatians 5:4, Paul was reminding them that they had been saved by grace. Thus it would be futile to attempt to live the Christian life by the works of keeping rules and regulations. The verse does not say that such persons have lost their salvation. Just as we have been saved by faith, we must live by faith (Gal. 3:11). Otherwise, we would lose the powerful effect Christ has in our lives.

Fifth, *but isn't there a verse in the Bible that talks about those who "fall away"?* This question likely refers to a very solemn passage of Scripture found in Hebrews. "For it is impossible for those who were once enlightened, and have tasted of the heavenly gift, and were made partakers of the Holy Ghost, And have tasted the good word of God, and the powers of the world to come, If they shall fall away, to renew them again unto repentance; seeing they crucify to themselves the Son of God afresh, and put him to an open shame" (Hebrews 6:4–6, KJV).

If this passage means that it is possible for a person to fall away after having been saved, then it must also teach that it is impossible for them to ever be renewed again unto repentance. That would mean that if you ever fell away once, then you could never be saved again. There are not many people who deny the validity of the eternal security of the believer who would be willing to accept that consequence.

Although this passage is difficult to interpret, many scholars believe that it may mean one of three things. Citing the use of the word "tasted," some would say that these persons had only "tasted" of the heavenly gift and had never really received it. They had come close to receiving Christ but had finally rejected the gospel and would never again be renewed unto repentance. Others believe that it means that a Christian can lose his or her opportunity for service and be placed on the shelf, never again to be used in the service of God. A third possible interpretation is that the writer suggests a hypothetical case, which is used to prove the impossibility of losing one's salvation.

Why This Doctrine Is Important

The doctrine of the security of the believer is tremendously important. Consider several reasons.

First, *it determines our view of salvation.* Is a person saved by works or by the grace of God? There really are only two kinds of religions in the world: the gospel of grace and all the others that rely on some system of works or achievement. If salvation depends on Jesus plus any thing else, it is not the gospel.

Second, *it determines our relationship to God.* Is God a Father who loves and keeps his children, or are we merely hired hands in God's employ? Our motivation for serving the Lord should not be our fear of the loss of our salvation but our love for him and our desire to please him.

Third, *it influences the work of the church.* If you can't be sure of your own salvation, much less the salvation of others that you bring to Christ, then the urgency of evangelism is diminished.

QUESTIONS

1. Why do people have such difficulty in accepting the doctrine of the eternal security of the believer?

2. What reasons did Jesus give in John 10:27–29 that his sheep are eternally secure?

3. What does 1 John 2:19 say about people who leave the Christian faith?

4. What do you think the term "fall away" means in Hebrews 6:6?

5. Why should the doctrine of the eternal security of the believer be an encouragement to live the Christian life?

6. What would you say to someone who is doubting his or her salvation?

Notes

1. W. T. Conner, *The Gospel of Redemption* (Nashville, Tennessee: Broadman Press, 1945), 247.

Soul Competency and the Priesthood of the Believer

BACKGROUND SCRIPTURES

Genesis 1:26–27; 2:7; Exodus 19:1–6; Psalm 8; 42:1–2;
Jeremiah 31:29–34; Ezekiel 18:1–4; Matthew 16:13–17;
John 3:1–16; 8:36; 14:12; Acts 4:12; 1 Corinthians 3:21,23;
Galatians 5:1,13; Ephesians 2:11–21; Hebrews 4:14–16; 8:8–13;
1 Peter 2:4–10; Revelation 5:1–10

FOCAL TEXTS

Genesis 1:26–27; Jeremiah 31:29–34; Matthew 16:16–17;
John 3:16; 1 Peter 2:4–10

MAIN IDEA

"There should be no institution, human person, rite, or system
which stands between the individual person and God. . . . All
have equal access to the Father's table, the Father's ear, and the
Father's heart."[1]

STUDY AIM

To identify implications of soul competency and the priesthood
of the believer

QUICK READ

Baptists believe in the priesthood of the believer and the soul
competency of a believer. We believe we relate to God without
human mediators, both as individuals and as a body of believers.

Religious freedom is a precious liberty. Baptists have battled legislatures, congresses, local authorities, and each other for the right of all people to worship, or not worship, God in their own way. The demand for religious liberty comes from the Baptist doctrines of soul competency and the priesthood of a believer or believers.

From Thomas Helwys to Roger Williams to George Truett, mainstream Baptist leaders have contended that each person bears responsibility for his or her relationship with God. An individual has the God-given competency to respond to God or not. An individual has the right and responsibility to interpret Scripture and apply biblical teachings to life. No authority has the power to coerce belief.

For generations Baptist laypeople and theologians, ministers and Sunday School teachers, have asserted these twin doctrines of right and responsibility. Some folks have even died to make the point that God gives every woman and man the competency to encounter the Lord, and that each believer has the responsibility to act as a priest before the Lord.

In the Beginning . . . (Genesis 1:26–27)

During the sixth creative event, according to Genesis 1:26–27, God made humans in the divine image. Then God gave the females and males "dominion" over everything else. What a sweeping statement and great responsibility!

Each time I teach Hebrew Bible to college freshmen, I ask the question, "How are we in God's image?" Sometimes they respond that we look like God, but I remind them that God is Spirit, and that the Hebrews condemned images and forbade making idols. With a bit of prompting, the students come up with some ways we reflect God's being. Consider these:

- Humans are rational beings. We can think, identify our emotions, make decisions, and accept responsibility.
- Women and men are religious beings. No matter what civilization

Genesis 1:26–27 (NRSV)

²⁶Then God said, "Let us make humankind in our image, according to our likeness; and let them have dominion over the fish of the sea, and over the birds of the air, and over the cattle, and over all the wild animals of the earth, and over every creeping thing that creeps upon the earth." ²⁷ So God created humankind in his image,
in the image of God he created them;
male and female he created them.

Jeremiah 31:29–34

²⁹ In those days they shall no longer say:
"The parents have eaten sour grapes,
and the children's teeth are set on edge."
³⁰But all shall die for their own sins; the teeth of everyone who eats sour grapes shall be set on edge.

³The days are surely coming, says the LORD, when I will make a new covenant with the house of Israel and the house of Judah. ³²It will not be like the covenant that I made with their ancestors when I took them by the hand to bring them out of the land of Egypt—a covenant that they broke, though I was their husband, says the LORD. ³³But this is the covenant that I will make with the house of Israel after those days, says the LORD: I will put my law within them, and I will write it on their hearts; and I will be their God, and they shall be my people. ³⁴No longer shall they teach one another, or say to each other, "Know the LORD," For they shall all know me, from the least of them to the greatest, says the LORD; for I will forgive their iniquity, and remember their sin no more.

Matthew 16:16–17

¹⁶Simon Peter answered, "You are the Messiah, the Son of the living God." ¹⁷And Jesus answered him, "Blessed are you, Simon son of Jonah! For flesh and blood has not revealed this to you, but my Father in heaven.

John 3:16

"For God so loved the world that he gave his only Son, so that everyone who believes in him may not perish but may have eternal life."

1 Peter 2:4–10

[4]Come to him, a living stone, though rejected by mortals yet chosen and precious in God's sight, and [5]like living stones, let yourselves be built into a spiritual house, to be a holy priesthood, to offer spiritual sacrifices acceptable to God through Jesus Christ. [6]For it stands in scripture:

> "See, I am laying in Zion a stone,
> a cornerstone chosen and precious;
> and whoever believes in him will not be put to shame."

[7]To you then who believe, he is precious; but for those who do not believe,

> "The stone that the builders rejected
> has become the very head of the corner,"

[8]and

> "A stone that makes them stumble,
> and a rock that makes them fall."

They stumble because they disobey the word, as they were destined to do.

[9]But you are a chosen race, a royal priesthood, a holy nation, God's own people, in order that you may proclaim the mighty acts of him who called you out of darkness into his marvelous light.

[10] Once you were not a people,
> but now you are God's people;
once you had not received mercy,
> but now you have received mercy.

an anthropologist finds or an archeologist digs up, that people group has a religion of some sort. They practice a religion.

• People are moral beings, recognizing good and evil. Cultures define "good" and "evil" differently, but all people have moral "slots" in their minds. Created in God's image, we think, make decisions, have religious yearnings, and have a sense of morality.

God gave us the capacity to make religious decisions, to recognize God's handiwork. God made us accountable for these abilities. God gave us soul competency because the Lord wanted uncoerced relationships to grow between ourselves and God.

Jesus modeled this doctrine for us. At no time in his ministry did he resort to force to make a point or coercion to create a positive response. In fact, when the disciples wanted to destroy an unfriendly village (Luke 9:51–56) and Peter cut off Malchus's ear (Matthew 26:47–55; John 18:10), Jesus rebuked the use of force to gain any spiritual end. True belief shines when people exercise their soul competency, when they use their God-given capacity to choose to follow God, not when someone suffers punishment if they don't conform religiously to a norm set by an authority. We have soul competency. God made us in the divine image, making us responsible for our decisions about relating to the Lord. No one can force true belief.

God Made a Promise . . . (Jeremiah 31:29–34)

The children of Israel lived with despair after the Babylonians took them into Exile and destroyed Jerusalem and the temple in 587 BC. Demoralized by their plight, the Hebrews asked tough questions. Has God deserted us? Can we worship God in this foreign place? Why did this happen?

God raised up prophets to help the Israelites answer these questions. One such prophet was Jeremiah of Anathoth. Jeremiah worked for more than forty years as a prophet in Judah. From the time of good King Josiah, through three Babylonian invasions, through an assassination attempt, Jeremiah wrestled with these questions. Through his writings, Jeremiah helped the Hebrews in Babylonia deal with their new life, and he affirmed God's presence with and care for the exiles. He affirmed that God had not deserted them, that they could worship God in Babylonia without the temple, and that their sin caused the destruction of Judah.

God gave Jeremiah a new insight into the way God wanted to relate to people. In Jeremiah 31:29–34, the prophet presented the New Covenant. Unlike the Mosaic Covenant, which the Law fleshed out for daily life and which focused on the creation of a Hebrew political state, the New Covenant emphasized the individual nature of religious commitment to God.

Thomas Helwys

In the early 1600s Thomas Helwys wrote a pamphlet titled *The Mystery of Iniquity*. In it he called for complete religious freedom in Great Britain. He presented a simple argument. Each person will stand before God and be judged alone. So, each individual must have the freedom to make spiritual decisions without coercion, because they will be judged for their choices. King James I sent Helwys to jail. The Baptist preacher died there.

What was most important to Helwys was not that he wrote the first plea for complete religious freedom published in England or that he served as pastor of the first Baptist church on English soil. What was most important to Helwys was that each person must relate to God individually in choosing to be a Christian, interpreting Scripture, and living a godly life under the direction of the Holy Spirit. Helwys paid dearly for his affirmation of the Baptist doctrine of soul competency and the priesthood of believers, but he considered it a price worth paying.

In verses 29–30, Jeremiah took the exiles to task for blaming their ancestors for their suffering. In traditional Hebrew life, the decisions of the head of the tribe affected all people in the clan. This corporate identity shifted with Jeremiah's firm insistence that each person is accountable to God for his or her own life. Community responsibility remained strong for the Hebrews, but spiritual life begins within the individual's decision regarding God. A parent can not choose God for a child, and neither can a child choose God for a parent. Each person, exercising soul competency, must choose or reject God by his or her own will.

With the New Covenant, God makes no promise regarding the creation of a political state. Rather, the promise concerns the spiritual state of each person. The Lord will inscribe the divine law on the hearts of believers, and they will know God. External sources can help clarify, explain, and teach, but it is in the personal relationship that God comes to a believer. Jeremiah does not minimize the importance of external influences in helping chart a person's spiritual growth. Rather the prophet stresses that the ultimate relationship is between God and the heart of a believer whose soul is competent to choose the Lord.

Fulfilled by Jesus . . . (Matthew 16:16–17; John 3:16)

Every major religion has priests. No matter what the religion, a priest has two functions: to lead in worship and to mediate between God and the world. The priest takes the world's needs to God and brings God's word to the world. Priests may function somewhat differently from religion to religion, but priests hold a special place in all religions.

Baptists teach that believers are priests. Each one has the responsibility to relate to God, to understand the Bible, and to interact with the Holy Spirit. We teach that God reveals God's self to each believer and that a Christian has the responsibility to respond to God's direction.

Matthew 16:16–17 illustrates this belief. Jesus withdrew from Jewish territory to rest and teach his closest followers on several occasions. One time they went to the resort town of Caesarea Philippi on a retreat, and Jesus posed the question (Matt. 16:13), "'Who do people say that the Son of Man is?'" After several different responses came from the disciples, Jesus asked, "'But who do you say that I am?'" Peter, the irrepressible, impetuous fisherman, blurted out, "You are the Messiah, the Son of the living God" (16:16).

I have heard many sermons on what Peter meant when he made that statement and on his faulty understanding of "messiah." Whatever Peter meant, Jesus complimented his statement by noting that God gave that insight to the fisherman. This text teaches many important truths about Jesus, messiahship, redemption, and courage. But it also underscores the Baptist doctrine of the priesthood of a believer. God dealt with Peter directly. The Lord did not go through a mediating human but went straight to the heart of the disciple and implanted truth.

We don't depend on mediators to bring God to us, because God comes to each of us in God's time and God's way. The Lord does use other believers to teach, heal, guide, and help us along our spiritual pathway. Our salvation, however, is not dependent on the actions of another human being. Our salvation depends only on God and our response to God. We are priests before the Lord, relating to God directly.

As a Journeyman missionary in Vietnam in 1973–1975, the first Scripture verse I memorized in Vietnamese was John 3:16. Years earlier I had learned it as a GA, and I had sung it in church choirs. But somehow, when I spoke the verse in Vietnamese, new meaning sprang from the text and imbedded itself in my heart.

An incredibly simple statement of the gospel, John 3:16 says it all. God did it; God did it perfectly; God did it with love; now, the responsibility rests with people to decide their response. This verse does not set up an elaborate hierarchy to mediate salvation or truth to the world. This verse states that the mediation is between Christ and the individual who believes. No middle-person comes on the scene. God sets a very simple criterion for salvation: belief. And we must decide what to do. We must go to God as believers and accept what God offers, depending only on God's promise fulfilled in the incarnation. If God keeps God's promises, we need no other mediator to be saved.

We Are Now God's Priests (1 Peter 2:4–10)

One of the things I do that brings me the most fun is to show students the beautiful ties between the Old and New Testaments, and how the early church picked up on so many of God's promises made before the time of Jesus. First Peter 2:4–10 models the marvelous continuity of Scripture. The passage also affirms an important variation of the Baptist doctrine of the priesthood of the believer.

The First Letter of Peter offered encouragement to Christians who suffered persecution for their faith. Ridiculed as idiots, immoral people, and troublemakers, the early believers suffered greatly at the hands of local officials as well as the Roman Empire. The letter gave comfort and encouragement to the hurting church members by rehearsing some of their religious history, and by showing how Jesus fulfilled prophecy they took very seriously. By drawing on the Old Testament, the letter gave validity to the church's claims that Jesus was Messiah, God in human form.

Case Study

You teach a Bible study class at your church. One of the members, a serious young Christian, has studied 1 Corinthians 11:5 and decided that the women of the church should wear head coverings. Given the doctrines of soul competency and the priesthood of believers, how would you deal with this situation? What would you say or suggest?

Verses 4–8 bring up familiar images: a stone rejected by a builder becoming a cornerstone and Christians as living stones being built into God's temple. These verses echo Paul's teaching in Ephesians 2:21–22. They also recite the Old Testament prophecies in Psalm 118:22; Isaiah 8:14; 28:16. God constructs the church from the individual building blocks of believers' lives. For persecuted believers, these words brought peace and hope, encouragement and comfort.

I always get excited when I have a chance to write or preach on 1 Peter 2:9–10, because these verses tie so wonderfully to God's promises from the Old Testament. In Exodus 19:5–6, God laid out the basic elements of the Mosaic Covenant for the Hebrew people. God made three promises to the Hebrews if they would obey the word of the Lord. If a Hebrew would keep God's commandments to show her or his love for the Lord, in return God would show divine love by keeping the three promises—to make of the Hebrew people a special treasure, a royal priesthood, and a holy nation.

Although we will focus on the "royal priesthood" promise, let's look quickly at the other two promises mentioned in both 1 Peter 2:9 and Exodus 19:5–6. God's chosen people, God's special treasure, alludes to a fact of ancient oriental life. A ruler owned everything in the realm—air, land, people, commerce. The ruler held it all for the next generation's use. The ruler, however, would have a "special treasure" that belonged to the monarch alone. The ruler could do with this "special treasure" whatever he or she wanted. Similarly, God created everything and owned all that existed, but the Hebrews constituted God's "special treasure."

God also promised to make the Hebrews a "holy nation" (1 Pet. 2:9; Ex. 19:5). To that end, God gave the Law so the Hebrews would know how to live. Being "holy" meant living a separated, pure life devoted to good. The rules found in the Old Testament provided guidelines for how to be a holy nation, how to separate themselves from their unbelieving neighbors. First Peter draws this theme from Exodus 19 and claims the church is God's holy nation now. Set apart by lifestyle and a desire for goodness and wholeness, believers live within God's commands given through the life and teaching of Jesus. To love God with everything and to love others as ourselves (Matthew 22:34–40)—these characteristics should define the "holy nation" of the church.

God promised in 1 Peter 2:9 (see Ex. 19:6) to make believers a "royal priesthood." For Baptists, the Lord fulfilled this promise by creating a community of faith. The church is the "new Israel" (see Galatians 6:16). Our doctrine affirms that as a community of faith we learn from each other, pray for each other, and mediate God to the world.

First Peter 2:9–10 teaches that the Christ-event fulfilled God's promise by making the church a priesthood of believers. Note the plural—*believers*. We are not lone rangers, on our own in the big, bad world. We are a people who have both individually and corporately related to God as priests. Thus, the body of Christ, through the priesthood of believers, mediates the world to God and God to the world. As good Baptists, we talk about this act with words like "evangelism" and "missions" rather than "mediation." But the intent is the same. By mediating God to the world, we seek to bring people to a point of exercising their soul competency to choose Christ. We also seek to mediate the needs of the world to God through prayer and responsible citizenship.

Are the concepts of priesthood of the believer and priesthood of the believers in conflict? No! One complements the other. As cooperating Baptists, we mediate God to the world through evangelism and missions, but as individual believers, we stand responsible before the Lord for our individual lives and actions in the church, in the home, and in the workplace. We mediate God to the world through how we live our lives and how we witness to the Lord. First Peter 2:4–10 contends that we are individuals responsible to and relating to God, but we also form a body of believers with responsibilities before the Lord. The two forms of priesthood complement one another, strengthen each other, and support the basic Baptist and Christian belief that God saves.

QUESTIONS

1. How does the priesthood of the believer work out in your life?

2. Does anyone, according to this Baptist doctrine, have the right to tell you what to believe or how to interpret the Bible?

3. How does your church function as a priesthood of believers?

4. What are some implications of the doctrine of soul competency for American politics?

Notes

1. Herschel H. Hobbs and E.Y. Mullins, *The Axioms of Religion*, rev. ed. (Nashville, Tennessee: Broadman Press, 1978), 75.

Symbolic Understanding of Baptism and the Lord's Supper

BACKGROUND SCRIPTURES

Matthew 3:13–17; 26:26–30; 28:18–20; Mark 1:9–11;
14:22–26; Luke 3:21–22; 22:14–20; John 3:23;
Acts 2:41–42; 8:35–39; 16:30–33; 20:7; Romans 6:1–7;
1 Corinthians 10:16,21; 11:23–29; Colossians 2:12

FOCAL TEXTS

Mark 1:9–11; Romans 6:1–7; 1 Corinthians 11:23–29

MAIN IDEA

"Christ instituted two ceremonial ordinances and committed
them to his people for perpetual observance—baptism and the
Lord's Supper. These two ceremonies are pictorial
representations of the fundamental facts of the gospel and of
our salvation through the gospel."[1]

STUDY AIM

To describe the Scriptural view of the nature of baptism and the
Lord's Supper

QUICK READ

The two ordinances, baptism and the Lord's Supper, tie Baptists
together by reminding them of the commitments they have
made to God and to one another.

When I returned to America after two years in Vietnam as a Missionary Journeyman, I wept the first time I heard the national anthem, and I got a lump in my throat the first time I saw the American flag flying in the breeze. The flag and the anthem are just symbols. But what power they possess!

Symbols play vital roles in our lives. Yet sometimes we forget how symbols shape our thoughts and actions. Never underestimate the power of a symbol, whether a symbol of national identity or of Baptist identity.

Baptists believe that the ordinances of the Lord's Supper and baptism are symbolic. As we consider this lesson, let us remember that Baptist doctrines fit together. Because we believe in salvation by grace, we also believe that baptism and the Lord's Supper do not save a person. No act you or I do saves us from our sin. But baptism and communion are powerful symbols of our faith, and we should take them seriously. Each ordinance says something about our covenant with Christ and with the church.

Baptism, a Symbol of Commitment (Mark 1:9–11)

We do well to look to the life of Jesus to begin understanding this doctrine. In Mark 1:9–11, the author recorded Jesus' baptism by John, his cousin. John, already acknowledged as a prophet, baptized folks in the Jordan River when they publicly repented of their sin and renewed their covenant with God. Baptism for Jews symbolized repentance and becoming part of the community of faith (see sidebar, "The Background of Baptism"). John offered serious people the opportunity to make a public statement about their relationship with God, a relationship that already existed.

When Jesus chose to be baptized, he made an important public statement. He did not need to repent of sin, because Jesus did not sin (Hebrews 4:15). Jesus identified with our human dilemma and made a

Mark 1:9–11 (NRSV)

9In those days Jesus came from Nazareth of Galilee and was baptized by John in the Jordan. 10And just as he was coming up out of the water, he saw the heavens torn apart and the Spirit descending like a dove on him. 11And a voice came from heaven, "You are my Son, the Beloved; with you I am well pleased."

Romans 6:1–7

1What then are we to say? Should we continue in sin in order that grace may abound? 2By no means! How can we who died to sin go on living in it? 3Do you not know that all of us who have been baptized into Christ Jesus were baptized into his death? 4Therefore we have been buried with him by baptism into death, so that, just as Christ was raised from the dead by the glory of the Father, so we too might walk in newness of life.

5For if we have been united with him in a death like his, we will certainly be united with him in a resurrection like his. 6We know that our old self was crucified with him so that the body of sin might be destroyed, and we might no longer be enslaved to sin. 7For whoever has died is freed from sin.

1 Corinthians 11:23–29

23For I received from the Lord what I also handed on to you, that the Lord Jesus on the night when he was betrayed took a loaf of bread, 24and when he had given thanks, he broke it and said, "This is my body that is for you. Do this in remembrance of me." 25In the same way he took the cup also, after supper, saying, "This cup is the new covenant in my blood. Do this, as often as you drink it, in remembrance of me." 26For as often as you eat this bread and drink the cup, you proclaim the Lord's death until he comes.

27Whoever, therefore, eats the bread or drinks the cup of the Lord in an unworthy manner will be answerable for the body and blood of the Lord. 28Examine yourselves, and only then eat of the bread and drink of the cup. 29For all who eat and drink without discerning the body, eat and drink judgment against themselves.

covenant with us and with God by his baptism. In Mark's account, the Holy Spirit descended on Jesus and a voice from heaven said, "You are my Son, the Beloved; with you I am well pleased" (Mark 1:11). For Jesus, baptism signified a covenant made and a relationship established between himself and humanity. He did not need salvation, but he did want to identify publicly with those committed to God.

Jesus accepted his role in the salvation process at his baptism. The voice from heaven put together parts of a psalm about the coming Messiah, the Promised One of Israel (Psalm 2:7), and the Servant (Isaiah 42:1) who would suffer and die for the salvation of the people. At his baptism, Jesus accepted the mantle of Messiah and Suffering Servant, two ideas that didn't flow together naturally within Judaism. Identifying with a sinning race and accepting his call, Jesus established the powerful nature of baptism as a symbol of commitment to God. Although not necessary for salvation, baptism became an important ritual of commitment to the way of God, and for humans, of turning from their old life to a new life with Christ.

Jews of Jesus' day believed in the symbolic nature of baptism. For the Jews, baptism was a symbol of entering the faith or of repentance and cleansing. However, at the time when Baptists began emerging from the Reformation in the 1600s, the general understanding of Christian baptism was that the act of baptism was part of salvation. A priest baptized babies to free them from the burden of original sin. Even in the Reformation traditions of Martin Luther and John Calvin, baptism remained more than symbol, and infants continued to be baptized into the church.

In the early 1600s, Baptists wrestled with who should be baptized and why. Baptists concluded that baptism symbolized a commitment to Christ already made and salvation already accepted. Thus, early Baptists baptized only adults who could make such a decision for Christ by themselves. In fact, as the new denomination grew, other Christians called the denomination "Baptist" because of Baptists' practice of adult believers' baptism and rejection of infant baptism. The process of understanding the role of baptism took decades. By 1644, however, when the

First London Confession was written by Baptists in that city, it clearly presented the symbolic nature of baptism:

> That Baptisme is an Ordinance of the new Testament given by Christ, to be dispensed onely upon persons professing faith, or that are Disciples, or taught, who upon profession of faith, ought to be baptized.[2]

Baptists today practice immersion when baptizing. At the beginning of the denomination's history, though, its leaders were not unanimous about the form of baptism. Accepting baptism as a symbol, Thomas Helwys, the pastor of the first Baptist church in England, felt okay with using affusion (flicking water from one's fingertips over the believer's head). Early Particular Baptists, those who believed Jesus died only for those "elected" to salvation, sprinkled believers. Particular Baptists adopted immersion as the correct form of baptism in the 1640s.

Immersion eventually became the standard form of baptism because the Greek verb *baptizo*, from which our word "baptize" comes, means "to immerse" (see sidebar, "The Background of Baptism"). As people who take Scripture seriously, Baptists identified immersion as the appropriate way to baptize people, because that is what the Bible says.

Death, Burial, and Resurrection (Romans 6:1–7)

Some folks think if an act is symbolic, it has no importance. Wrong! Baptism and the Lord's Supper are symbols, but they remain critically important to the identity of Baptists and of Christians generally. Paul thought they held great importance for the early Church and for all believers.

Paul wrote the Letter to the Romans to introduce himself to that church. He had not visited the congregation. He knew, though, of their work in the Imperial City, and they knew of his work in the provinces. Paul intended to ask for the Romans' help to make a missionary journey

The Background of Baptism

When the translators of the King James Version of the Bible came to the Greek verb *baptizo*, they had trouble. The verb means "to dip, to plunge, to immerse under water." Because the Church of England sprinkled as the rite of entry into the church, the scholars faced a problem—how to translate the verb. They solved the problem by not translating the word *baptizo*. The scholars simply brought the verb into the English language as *baptize*.

The biblical form of baptism parallels the form one experienced to become an adult convert to Judaism. Being immersed to become a Jew symbolized death to the old life and cleansing for the new life. To become a Jew, a person underwent several immersions over a period of time, but the early Christians adopted one immersion as sufficient.

The symbolism in Judaism carried over to Christianity—death, burial, and resurrection; cleansing from sin to a pure life. For the Hebrews and for Baptists, baptism is not magical and carries no power of its own, but it symbolizes a very important reality.

to Spain. To enlist their aid, he wrote the Letter of Romans to explain his beliefs and commitments. He included theological insights he felt critical to the Christian faith. Of all his letters, the one to the Roman church presents most fully what Paul believed and taught. To this book we turn to gain insight into Paul's position on the importance of baptism, looking particularly at Romans 6:1–7.

As discussed in the lesson on salvation by grace, Baptists believe that the process of salvation includes salvation from the punishment for sin (regeneration), current salvation from the power of sin (sanctification), and future salvation from the presence of sin (glorification). In Romans 6:1–7, Paul talked about these three facets of salvation and tied each one to baptism, not just baptism with water, but baptism into the life of Christ.

Dealing with the important topic of freedom from sin, Paul used powerful imagery to explain how a Christian relates to the salvation event and process. We as baptized believers share in Christ's death, burial, and resurrection. Paul explained how baptism symbolizes burial of our old selves with Christ's burial and our emergence into "newness of life" as we came out of the water (Romans 6:4). For Paul, the act of baptism meant our identification with Christ publicly, with the sorrow of his death, but also with the power of his resurrection. What hope Paul extended to us as he struggled to understand and communicate the meaning of the Christ-event!

Paul piled on promise after promise symbolized by baptism. We share Christ's death; we share Christ's burial; we share Christ's resurrection; we share the glory of Christ. No longer bound by sin, we live a new life, one powered by our commitment to God. But we also live this life in community with other believers. Baptism is a public event, a public commitment to the Lordship of Christ, a public identification with the community of faith. Paul taught that with this one act of baptism, the purpose and power of the Incarnation became clear to everyone viewing the baptism or participating in the act itself.

My church celebrates baptisms at the beginning of Sunday morning worship, and our ministers take turns officiating. One Sunday, when the youth minister baptized a couple of young people, she said something that struck me. I hadn't thought about the promise the church makes to the person being baptized. As Susan lowered and raised each young person, she reminded the congregation that as these new church members made promises to us about their commitment to Christ, we made a promise to them to help nurture and "grow" them in the faith. For the first time in a long time, the power of the symbol held me—death, burial, resurrection in Christ, *and* a commitment to the body of Christ.

Paul wrote to the church at Rome, not just to individuals who happened to hear the letter read at a worship service. For Baptists, the public act of baptism of believers by immersion signifies the commitment already made by the individual. It also symbolizes the covenant made by the congregation with the new member and with God. Jesus identified with us through baptism, and we identify with Jesus and one another through baptism. Just a symbol? Yes, but so much more, too.

Communion and Community (1 Corinthians 11:23–29)

I grew up in Southern Baptist churches from Hawaii to Virginia. Dad served in the Marine Corps. So I experienced many ways of celebrating communion. But almost always, the Lord's Supper got tacked onto the morning service or the evening service. I felt like the ministers said, "Oops, it's the end of the quarter, and we have to celebrate the Lord's Supper." I liked the grape juice a lot, but the crackers usually didn't taste very good. I had friends, members of other denominations, who had communion every Sunday. I decided it would be really boring to have to go through this stuff every week. Since that time, after studying the reason we celebrate the Lord's Supper, I realize that as an immature Christian, I was so very, very wrong to think of communion as boring.

Paul wrote the oldest description of the Lord's Supper in his First Letter to the Corinthian church. For the apostle, communion gave the church a specific, designated time to reflect on the price of our salvation. The Lord's Supper focused hearts and minds on what Jesus endured in order for believers to experience God's saving grace. "Do this in remembrance of me" (1 Corinthians 11:24). Each time we partake of communion, we remember Jesus' sacrifice on our behalf. Too, we have an opportunity to examine our hearts and take care of any unfinished business between ourselves and God. Only a symbol—but one that has the power to confront us with our spiritual need.

In 1 Corinthians 11:23–29, the apostle laid down the "elements" for celebrating communion—"a loaf of bread," "the cup," spiritual self-examination, and a community of faith. Interpreting the Lord's Supper as symbolic and not necessary for salvation, Baptists' celebration of communion includes these elements in one form or another. Through the years, we have argued over whether to use wine or grape juice to represent Christ's blood. We have argued over whether to use unleavened bread or broken crackers to represent Christ's broken body. Should we use individual cups? Should we make everyone come to the front to take the elements? Should we break the bread up first or let everyone take a chunk on their own? In fact, perhaps we argued so much over the details of communion that we sometimes forgot the *point* of the Lord's Supper—that Jesus' body was broken for us, that Jesus' blood was shed for us.

Self-examination is also part of communion. Have you ever refused to participate in the Lord's Supper because of your spiritual condition? Do we think about the current state of our soul as we pass the bread and juice? Now and then, something forces me to assess my spiritual condition during communion. When I do, the time of worship becomes more meaningful. This symbol of Christ's sacrifice highlights the petty nature of most of my spiritual complaints. This symbol blows away the smoke I wrap around my sin to hide it from God. This symbol provides me with the time to respond anew to God's grace with repentance for my current spiritual failures.

Paul came down hard on people who breezed by the self-examination part of communion. In verse 29, he wrote that folks who blithely take the Lord's Supper with no thought for their own relationship with God "eat and drink judgment against themselves." I have no idea what that means in eternal terms, but it sounds bad! In my own life, I know that when I ignore the need to "get right with God," I suffer a sense of separation I don't like. Should we take more seriously Paul's command to examine ourselves, and "only then eat of the bread and drink of the cup" (11:28). Food for thought.

Historically, Baptists recognize communion as an activity of the body of Christ, the community of faith. Jesus shared the bread and the cup in the upper room with the community of the Twelve. We share the bread and cup with our community of faith. If your church has a ministry that takes the Lord's Supper to homebound members, why do you do this? You do it to strengthen the homebound person's sense of "oneness" with the congregation by sharing communion. I suppose it's possible for one person to celebrate the Lord's Supper and find it meaningful, but the presence of like-minded sisters and brothers in Christ makes the celebration much more powerful. Whether grape juice or wine, whether bread or crackers, the symbol of communion gains strength when shared within the body of Christ.

Some Baptists disagree about who should participate in the celebration of communion in the local church. Some folks think anyone confessing Christ as Lord qualifies for the celebration. Others think only Baptists should participate in the Lord's Supper. Still others include only members of that local Baptist church in the celebration. Historically, Baptists were all over the map on this issue. English Baptists argued in the 1700s over whether they should include John Bunyan's church in their fellowship, because he served communion to any Christian. In America, the Landmark movement leaders of the 1800s protested that only local church members should take communion.

According to Baptist doctrine, each congregation must decide whom to include and whom to exclude when celebrating the Lord's Supper. I would suppose, however, that when we get to heaven, God will have no

Case Study

You have a good Christian friend visiting from out of town. This friend goes to church with you on the Sunday that your congregation celebrates the Lord's Supper. Your friend is a Methodist and wants to participate in the Lord's Supper. What do you tell your friend? What do *you* think about the issue?

restrictions on which of the residents of heaven can come to the heavenly table.

Taking the Symbols Seriously

Baptism and the Lord's Supper are two powerful symbols of our individual and corporate relationship with God. All of us need to take these celebrations more seriously and more thoughtfully. As Baptists we affirm their importance. As Baptists, let us take our own affirmation to heart and take these two ordinances more seriously.

QUESTIONS

1. What is most meaningful to you about baptism?

2. What is most meaningful to you about the Lord's Supper?

3. What might your church do to enhance the meaningfulness of the celebration of the two ordinances?

4. Do you feel uncomfortable when attending another church that does communion or baptism differently? Why?

Notes

1. Walter Thomas Conner, *Christian Doctrine* (Nashville, Tennessee: Broadman Press, 1937), 273.
2. William L. Lumpkin, *Baptist Confessions of Faith*, rev. ed. (Valley Forge: Judson Press, 1969), 167.

Voluntary Cooperation Among Churches

BACKGROUND SCRIPTURES

Acts 15; Galatians 2; 2 Corinthians 8—9

FOCAL TEXTS

Acts 15:1–2, 22–32; Galatians 2:1–10;
2 Corinthians 8:1–8, 16—9:6

MAIN IDEA

"That the churches in the New Testament were local autonomous bodies under the lordship of Christ is quite clear. At the same time there is the pattern of voluntary cooperation between churches in matters of mutual interest and concern."[1]

STUDY AIM

To describe the New Testament pattern Baptists follow in relationships with fellow churches

QUICK READ

While Baptist churches are independent, autonomous, and diverse in membership and ministry, we have a great desire to cooperate together to advance the cause of Christ.

Two bedrock convictions of Baptists are the priesthood of every believer
and the autonomy and independence of every New Testament church.
For centuries Baptists have rejected the priestly system and the hierarchical and presbyterial forms of church government.

Baptists have believed in the direct access of each believer to the
throne of mercy to find grace and help in time of need without any
human intermediary. They further have believed that the only "head" of
any church is none other than Jesus Christ. No local church is answerable
to any other body on earth and should not be ruled by any internal or
external hierarchy or presbytery.

Some Baptists have taken that to mean that they are forbidden to work
together with any other group but their own local churches. By shear
numbers, however, it can be demonstrated that most Baptists like to work
together with others of like faith and order. They prefer cooperation but
absolutely reject coercion in any form.

Cooperative Missions (Acts 15:1–2, 22–33)

This passage describes the first meeting of more than one local church to
discuss subjects of spiritual concern. The matters considered are not as
relevant to this particular study as the manner in which the issues were
settled.

Acts 13—14 recounts the bold mission adventure and exciting results
of the first missionary journey of Paul and Barnabas. When they returned
to Antioch they gathered the church together and gave a report of how
God "had opened a door of faith to the Gentiles" (Acts 12:27). Everyone
in the church must have been thrilled and excited.

But some men came down from Judea and began teaching that a person cannot be saved without following the Jewish ritual of circumcision
(15:1). Paul and Barnabas disagreed vehemently with this return to legalism. They debated the visiting Judaizers (15:2). The Judaizers were people of Jewish background within the Christian church who believed that
Gentiles first had to become Jews and keep the Jewish laws and rituals

Acts 15:1-2, 22-32 (NASB)

[1]Some men came down from Judea and began teaching the brethren, "Unless you are circumcised according to the custom of Moses, you cannot be saved." [2]And when Paul and Barnabas had great dissension and debate with them, the brethren determined that Paul and Barnabas and some others of them should go up to Jerusalem to the apostles and elders concerning this issue.

• •

[22]Then it seemed good to the apostles and the elders, with the whole church, to choose men from among them to send to Antioch with Paul and Barnabas—Judas called Barsabbas, and Silas, leading men among the brethren, [23]and they sent this letter by them,

"The apostles and the brethren who are elders, to the brethren in Antioch and Syria and Cilicia who are from the Gentiles, greetings. [24]"Since we have heard that some of our number to whom we gave no instruction have disturbed you with their words, unsettling your souls, [25]it seemed good to us, having become of one mind, to select men to send to you with our beloved Barnabas and Paul, [26]men who have risked their lives for the name of our Lord Jesus Christ. [27]"Therefore we have sent Judas and Silas, who themselves will also report the same things by word of mouth. [28]"For it seemed good to the Holy Spirit and to us to lay upon you no greater burden than these essentials: [29]that you abstain from things sacrificed to idols and from blood and from things strangled and from fornication; if you keep yourselves free from such things, you will do well. Farewell."

[30]So when they were sent away, they went down to Antioch; and having gathered the congregation together, they delivered the letter. [31]When they had read it, they rejoiced because of its encouragement. [32]Judas and Silas, also being prophets themselves, encouraged and strengthened the brethren with a lengthy message.

Galatians 2:1-10

[1]Then after an interval of fourteen years I went up again to Jerusalem with Barnabas, taking Titus along also. [2]It was because of a revelation that I went up; and I submitted to them the gospel which I preach among the Gentiles, but I did so in private to those who were of reputation, for fear that I might be running, or had run, in vain. [3]But not even Titus, who was with me, though he was a Greek, was compelled to be circumcised. [4]But it was because of the false brethren secretly brought in, who had sneaked in to spy out our liberty which we have in Christ Jesus, in order to bring us into bondage. [5]But we did not yield in subjection to them for even an hour, so that the truth of the gospel would remain with you. [6]But from those who were of high reputation (what they were makes no difference to me; God shows no partiality)—well, those who were of reputation contributed nothing to me. [7]But on the contrary, seeing that I had been entrusted with the gospel to the uncircumcised, just as Peter had been to the circumcised [8](for He who effectually worked for Peter in his apostleship to the circumcised effectually worked for me also to the Gentiles), [9]and recognizing the grace that had been given to me, James and Cephas and John, who were reputed to be pillars, gave to me and Barnabas the right hand of fellowship, so that we might go to the Gentiles and they to the circumcised. [10]They only asked us to remember the poor—the very thing I also was eager to do.

before they could become Christians. To deal with the disturbance brought about by the Judaizers, the church members decided that Paul and Barnabas should go to Jerusalem and settle the issue (15:3).

The church at Antioch had not sought permission from the church at Jerusalem to send Paul and Barnabas on their missionary journey. So it is obvious that they did not assume that the church in Jerusalem was in authority over them. However, they had a desire to confer with the Jerusalem church to prevent a schism in the ranks and to share the obvious movement of God among the Gentiles.

2 Corinthians 8:1-8, 16-24

¹Now, brethren, we wish to make known to you the grace of God which has been given in the churches of Macedonia, ²that in a great ordeal of affliction their abundance of joy and their deep poverty overflowed in the wealth of their liberality. ³For I testify that according to their ability, and beyond their ability, they gave of their own accord, ⁴begging us with much urging for the favor of participation in the support of the saints, ⁵and this, not as we had expected, but they first gave themselves to the Lord and to us by the will of God. ⁶So we urged Titus that as he had previously made a beginning, so he would also complete in you this gracious work as well.

⁷But just as you abound in everything, in faith and utterance and knowledge and in all earnestness and in the love we inspired in you, see that you abound in this gracious work also. ⁸I am not speaking this as a command, but as proving through the earnestness of others the sincerity of your love also.

• •

¹⁶But thanks be to God who puts the same earnestness on your behalf in the heart of Titus. ¹⁷For he not only accepted our appeal, but being himself very earnest, he has gone to you of his own accord. ¹⁸We have sent along with him the brother whose fame in the things of the gospel has spread through all the churches; ¹⁹and not only this, but he has also been appointed by the churches to travel with us in this gracious work, which is being administered by us for the glory of the Lord Himself, and to show our readiness, ²⁰taking precaution so that no one will discredit us in our administration of this generous gift; ²¹for we have regard for what is honorable, not only in the sight of the Lord, but also in the sight of men. ²²We have sent with them our brother, whom we have often tested and found diligent in many things, but now even more diligent because of his great confidence in you. ²³As for Titus, he is my partner and fellow worker among you; as for our brethren, they are messengers of the churches, a glory to Christ. ²⁴Therefore openly before the churches, show them the proof of your love and of our reason for boasting about you.

2 Corinthians 9:1-6

[1]For it is superfluous for me to write to you about this ministry to the saints; [2]for I know your readiness, of which I boast about you to the Macedonians, namely, that Achaia has been prepared since last year, and your zeal has stirred up most of them. [3]But I have sent the brethren, in order that our boasting about you may not be made empty in this case, so that, as I was saying, you may be prepared; [4]otherwise if any Macedonians come with me and find you unprepared, we—not to speak of you—will be put to shame by this confidence. [5]So I thought it necessary to urge the brethren that they would go on ahead to you and arrange beforehand your previously promised bountiful gift, so that the same would be ready as a bountiful gift and not affected by covetousness.

[6]Now this I say, he who sows sparingly will also reap sparingly, and he who sows bountifully will also reap bountifully.

Although the churches were separate and autonomous, they desired to have strong ties of fellowship. Anyone who knows anything about the life of Paul would know that he most assuredly did not go to Jerusalem to "get permission" for Gentiles to be saved!

After the two missionaries arrived in Jerusalem, it became known that some of the Pharisees who had become followers of Christ did not believe Gentiles could be saved without first becoming Jewish proselytes (15:5). Steeped in Judaistic legalism, it was difficult for them to understand that salvation was by grace and available to Jew and Gentile alike.

Paul and Barnabas seem to have kept a low profile in the discussions. Simon Peter recounted again his experience with the household of Cornelius (Acts 10). On that occasion the Gentiles were so obviously saved that no one could deny it. He further made the point that there was only one pattern of salvation and not two. Peter clearly maintained that all must be saved through the grace of the Lord Jesus Christ (15:11). Then Paul and Barnabas gave an account of the mighty acts of God that had been done among the Gentiles (15:12).

Evidently James, half brother of the Lord, as pastor of the church served as moderator of the meeting. When the discussion was over, James cited several Old Testament prophecies that Gentiles would seek the Lord (15:15–18). He then gave his own personal "judgment" on the subject along with a few words of advice (15:19–21). His conclusion was that the Gentiles who were turning to God should not be troubled, but that the Gentile converts should be sensitive to the feelings of the Jewish people.

When James said, "It is my judgment" (15:19), he did not mean that he was a judge issuing his verdict. Rather he meant that he was sharing his best judgement on the matter with the assembled group for their response. The apostles, elders, and the whole church participated in the decision. Some of the leaders were chosen to hand-deliver a letter to the church at Antioch from the council that had convened in Jerusalem (15:22). Judas, called Barsabbas, and Silas were selected to represent the Jerusalem brethren at Antioch.

The text of the letter is contained in Acts 15:23–29. The letter begins with a greeting not only to the church in Antioch but also to the Gentile Christians in Syria and Cilicia (15:23). The official letter from no less than the apostles and the brethren disavowed the mission of the men who had disturbed the new Gentile Christians. The church had neither sent nor instructed them (15:24).

The unified opinion of the group was mentioned so that the churches at Antioch would be encouraged to know that the matter was settled and that there was no disagreement among them. Both Barnabas and Paul were called "our beloved" and were affirmed and admired for having "risked their lives" for the name of our Lord Jesus Christ (15:25–26).

The purpose of the mission of Judas and Silas was to report by word of mouth the same things that were written on the paper, and no doubt, to answer any questions. Plain words written on cold parchment could be misunderstood. It was good for someone to go along and share the demeanor, tone of voice, and gentle spirit that was intended (15:27). The leadership of the Holy Spirit is acknowledged as the foundation of the response that is being made to the Gentile Christians (15:28).

Because of the *diaspora* (the spread of the Jewish people beyond the land of Israel), there were Jews and synagogues scattered all over the Roman world (15:21). The Gentile Christians were asked to abstain from things sacrificed to idols, from blood, from things strangled, and from fornication, which was so rampant in pagan worship (15:29). Gentile Christians should be sensitive to the deep-seated customs and high moral standards of the Jews. At the same time, Jewish Christians should not burden Gentiles with rituals and regulations.

When the group arrived in Antioch, the whole congregation gathered together to hear the reading of the letter (15:30). When they heard it, there was great rejoicing, and they were all encouraged by it (15:31).

Judas and Silas were also prophets (preachers) and "encouraged" (or "exhorted," KJV) and strengthened the brethren "with a lengthy message"—just like preachers (15:32)! Under the inspiration of the occasion

Cooperation

Christ's people should, as occasion requires, organize such associations and conventions as may best secure cooperation for the great objects of the Kingdom of God. Such organizations have no authority over one another or over the churches. They are voluntary and advisory bodies designed to elicit, combine, and direct the energies of our people in the most effective manner. Members of New Testament churches should cooperate with one another in carrying forward the missionary, educational, and benevolent ministries for the extension of Christ's Kingdom. Christian unity in the New Testament sense is spiritual harmony and voluntary cooperation for common ends by various groups of Christ's people. Cooperation is desirable between the various Christian denominations, when the end to be attained is itself justified, and when such cooperation involves no violation of conscience or compromise of loyalty to Christ and His Word as revealed in the New Testament.

—ARTICLE 14, "THE BAPTIST FAITH AND MESSAGE," 1963

the two preachers were exhorting and strengthening these Gentile Christians in the faith.

Bible commentator W. Graham Scroggie has a wonderful comment on Acts 15:

> We should learn from this conference that it is well for brethren to confer, and endeavor to see one another's view-point, and well is it, also, that we should be willing, in the interests of Christian concord to yield something, whenever we can do so without the sacrifice of principle. . . . It is not to be expected that all Christians will ever see alike on all matters, nor is it desirable, but it is always possible while holding our particular view, to have the fullest fellowship for those from whom we differ. . . . Christianity is a religion of freedom and not of bondage, of peace and not of strife, of love and not of ill will."[2]

Voluntary Cooperation (Galatians 2:1–10)

The Letter to the Galatians provides another illustration of the voluntary cooperation of autonomous churches. Galatians was written by the Apostle Paul to encourage the Gentile Christians who had been confused by the efforts of the Judaizers. The Judaizers had given the message to the Galatian Christians that Gentiles had to keep the Jewish laws and rituals to become Christians. The previous passage in Acts 15 describes the events that took place at the Jerusalem conference. This passage shows the "damage control" that Paul attempted to do among the Gentile churches as the conflict continued.

Paul stoutly maintained that he had received the gospel through a revelation of Jesus Christ, not from the apostles in Jerusalem (Galatians 1:11–12, 15–17). He said, "We did not yield in subjection to them for even an hour, so that the truth of the gospel would remain with you" (2:5). Paul and Barnabas presented their gospel message to people known as the "pillars" of the church—James (the half brother of Jesus), Peter, and John (2:2, 9). They then gave Paul and Barnabas the "right hand of fellowship" (2:9).

Paul said that they were specifically asked to remember the poor, which he was very eager to do (2:10). Indeed, Paul had already been part of a delegation some years before who had taken a special offering for hunger relief from the church in Antioch to the Christians in Judea (Act 11:27–30).

In this account some very important issues concerning cooperative efforts among New Testament Christians are clarified.

- Cooperation was voluntary. Not even the "mother church" in Jerusalem, not Peter and John, and not even James, the half brother of the Lord himself, exercised hierarchical powers over Paul or the mission efforts of the church in Antioch.

- Paul voluntarily submitted himself to his fellow Christians in the interest of maintaining the fellowship of the Christian community. Greek scholar A. T. Robertson called the right hand of fellowship the "dramatic and concluding act of the pact for cooperation and coordinate, independent spheres of activity. The compromisors and the Judaizers were brushed to one side when these five men shook hands as equals in the work of Christ's Kingdom."[3]

- The word translated "fellowship" (2:9) is the Greek word *koinonia*. The word refers to "partnership." The Christian community has a partnership together in the gospel enterprise. By such joint efforts churches are able to do together far more than any one of them could ever do alone. This "gospel partnership" extended at least to missions, ministries, and hunger relief in the New Testament. Pulling together the smallest churches can do more for the cause of Christ than a mega-church can do alone. From many tiny raindrops, a great river flows.

Cooperative Giving (2 Corinthians 8:1–8, 16—9:6)

In this passage Paul commended the Macedonian churches for their generosity in giving an offering to help the churches in Jerusalem. He also explained to the church at Corinth the financial safeguards that had been

"Particular Baptists of the Old School"

The "Particular Baptists of the Old School" convened at Black Rock, Maryland, September 28, 1832. They unanimously approved a committee report that stated their objections to some "modern inventions."

Among these "modern inventions" were Sunday Schools, colleges and theological schools, cooperation in mission work, and meetings aimed at winning the lost. Little wonder that this group has long ago passed out of existence.

put into place. Further, he strongly encouraged the Corinthian church to give the offering previously promised.

Paul pointed to several reasons for the church at Corinth to give to the offering in cooperation with fellow believers. He first emphasized the greatest example of sacrificial giving, the Lord Jesus: " . . . Though He was rich, yet for your sake He became poor, so that you through His poverty might become rich" (2 Corinthians 8:9).

Paul also referred to the example of the Macedonian churches. The Macedonian churches would include Thessalonica, Berea, and Philippi. Paul may well have been at Philippi as he wrote this letter. The spirit and conduct of these churches continue to be a source of inspiration to us today. Although they were in "a great ordeal of affliction," they possessed an "abundance of joy" (8:2). In spite of the "deep poverty" they were experiencing, they "overflowed in the wealth of their liberality" (8:2). How could these churches have given in such a manner? Giving is more a matter of the heart than the pocket book. The secret was that they had first given themselves to the Lord (8:5).

Apparently Paul had been reluctant to receive an offering from Macedonia, given the dire circumstances of those churches. He wrote, however, that they were "begging us with much urging for the favor of participation in the support of the saints" (8:4). Perhaps the contemporary spirit of our age today is illustrated by the television program, *Greed*. On that program, the recurring thematic question is, "Do you have a need for greed?" Christians have exactly the opposite need. We have a need to give joyfully for the furtherance of the gospel.

Note the word "participation" in verse 4. The Greek word for "participation" in this verse is, again, a form of the word *koinonia*. As indicated in discussing Galatians 2:9, a basic meaning of this word is "partnership." Just because the Macedonian Christians were poor, they did not want to be denied the privilege of investing in the gospel partnership. No wonder Paul could write to the Philippian Christians, "I thank my God in all my remembrance of you . . . thankful for your partnership in the gospel from the first day until now" (Philippians 1:3, 5 RSV[4]). Partners have both responsibilities and rewards. Spiritual investments in time will yield dividends for all eternity (see Phil. 4:17).

Note that Paul was sensitive to the need for strict accountability for the use of the funds that had been given so sacrificially. Representatives of each participating church were sent to see that the offerings were used for their intended purpose (2 Cor. 8:20–23).

Generosity in cooperative mission giving is encouraged. The offering was so large that it evidently required an entire year to get it all together (9:2). All giving to the Lord should be done cheerfully and generously, not

The "Voluntary Principle"

"Churches may sometimes best carry out their mission by a combination of efforts. . . . Mission boards, associations, and conventions of all kinds represent such co-operative effort on the part of individual Christians and churches.

"In all such movements it should be remembered that the voluntary principle should be maintained for both the individual and the church, and the independence of the local churches should be strictly safeguarded."[5]

grudgingly (9:6–7). Any farmer who is stingy with his seed by seeing how little he can sow and how much he can keep back will have a very small harvest. The farmer "who sows bountifully shall also reap bountifully" (9:6).

Our Work Together

Just as there are many different kinds of people in the body of Christ, there are also many different kinds of Baptist churches. The members of the churches are gifted in many different ways to profit the whole body (see 1 Corinthians 12:4–7).

For the very same reason, all kinds of Baptist churches are needed to reach an increasing diversity of peoples and to provide an increased variety of ministries. Diversity is good. We should neither expect nor desire that all churches will be exactly alike. One of the first principles of voluntary cooperation among the churches is that diversity is desirable.

Another important principle is that because we have one Head over all the churches, we ought to have unity in the midst of our diversity. We should celebrate our diversity but also preserve diligently our unity. We do not all have to be alike as long as we have "one Lord, one faith, one baptism, one God and Father of all who is over all and through all and in all" (Ephesians 4:5–6). We Baptists (and all Christians) are entreated "to walk in a manner worthy of the calling with which you have been called, with all humility and gentleness, with patience, showing tolerance for one another in love, being diligent to preserve the unity of the Spirit in the bond of peace" (Eph. 4:1–3).

We can do many times more together than we ever could separately. The impact of the whole is greater than the sum of its parts! By joining hearts and hands we can provide more ministries, hospitals, universities, children's homes, ministerial education, mission support, church encouragement, and assistance than separate churches could ever supply. A rope of a thousand strands is stronger than a thousand single strands.

The motivation for this voluntary cooperation is that we love and serve the same Lord. How can people who are so diverse, so fiercely independent, so completely democratic, cooperate without coercion in such an effective way? This is one of the wonders of the entire religious world. Maybe we are like the ant, "which, having no chief, officer or ruler, prepares her food in the summer and gathers her provision in the harvest" (Proverbs 6:7–8). Individually we may be like the tiny ant, but collectively working together, each one doing his or her part, we can exert a powerful influence in the world for good and for God.

QUESTIONS

1. Why is diversity desirable among Baptist churches?

2. What did Jesus do to become the greatest of all examples of Christian giving?

3. Why is the tiny ant a good example of voluntary cooperation?

4. What did Paul do to ensure accountability for the offerings given?

5. Why do you think most Baptists want to voluntarily cooperate together?

Notes

1. Herschel H. Hobbs and E.Y. Mullins, *The Axioms of Religion*, rev. ed. (Nashville, Tennessee: Broadman Press, 1978), 107.
2. W. G. Scroggie, *The Acts of the Apostles* (Grand Rapids, Michigan: Zondervan Publishing House, 1976), 116–117.
3. A. T. Robertson, *Word Pictures in the New Testament*, vol. 4 (Nashville, Tennessee: Broadman Press, 1931), 286.
4. Scripture marked RSV is from the Holy Bible, Revised Standard Version, copyright 1946, 1952, Division of Christian Education of the National Council of the Churches of Christ in the United States of America.
5. W. T. Conner, *Christian Doctrine* (Nashville, Tennessee: Broadman Press, 1937), 270.